Living Past the Lies.

Living Past the Lies.

6-WEEK BIBLE STUDY

*Who You Are,
How You're Loved &
Why You're Created*

SHANNON DAWSON

Copyright © 2019 by Shannon Dawson.

All rights reserved. No part of this publication may be reproduced, distributed, or transmitted in any form or by any means, including photocopying, recording, or other electronic or mechanical methods, without the prior written permission of the publisher, except in the case of brief quotations embodied in critical reviews and certain other noncommercial uses permitted by copyright law. For permission requests, write to the publisher at the address below.

Fedd Books
P.O. Box 341973
Austin, TX 78734

www.thefeddagency.com

Published in association with The Fedd Agency, Inc., a literary agency.

Unless otherwise noted, all scripture quotations are from the ESV® Bible (The Holy Bible, English Standard Version®), copyright © 2001 by Crossway, a publishing ministry of Good News Publishers. Used by permission. All rights reserved.

Scripture quotations marked (NLT) are taken from the Holy Bible, New Living Translation, copyright ©1996, 2004, 2015 by Tyndale House Foundation. Used by permission of Tyndale House Publishers, Inc., Carol Stream, Illinois 60188. All rights reserved.

ISBN: 978-1-949784-06-0
eISBN: 978-1-949784-07-7

Printed in the United States of America

First Edition 15 14 13 12 11 / 10 9 8 7 6 5 4 3 2

Table of Contents

Introduction..9

Before You Begin..15

Week One: "You Are Not Enough"..21

Week Two: "Don't Look Back"..49

Week Three: "You Need It"...81

Week Four: "You Have to Fit In"..111

Week Five: "You Just Need to Think Positively"........................135

Week Six: "You Are Unlovable"...167

Conclusion..189

Leading Your Own Bible Study...199

Acknowledgments..205

Endnotes..207

Notes..208

This book is dedicated to my loving husband, Phil, who saw more in me than I ever saw in myself. To my three amazing, talented, and God-fearing children. Lastly, to my parents, Ken and Billie—thank you for the love you've shown to me, your commitment to Christ, and the example you set of how to serve others. My heart is full because of God and you!

Introduction

Hi, I'm Shannon Dawson and I'm so thankful you've picked up my Bible Study. I've never pretended to be a Bible expert. I've never been to seminary and I don't have a degree in theology, but I've spent years reading and studying my battered, old Bible and I love God. A lot. I want you to have the chance to know and love Him too.

So, who am I? (Besides not a theologian!?) I'm a wife to an incredible, godly man named Phil Dawson, who I am still head over heels in love with two decades after our wedding. Phil has been an NFL kicker for over twenty-one years, so I've been an NFL wife for all of that time and I'm so thankful for the life we've been blessed with as a result. I'm a mom to three amazing kids. I spend my days ferrying them from activity to activity, doing laundry, packing lunches, running errands, constantly losing my keys, and occasionally covering my gray hairs with a Sharpie! I'm also the adopted daughter of a preacher and his wife, and, consequently, raised on a tight budget and cans of SPAM and Spaghetti-Os. Vacations growing up meant long drives to visit my aunt and uncle; facing backwards in our wood-paneled, Griswold-green station wagon; and coming home with a farmer's tan, dirty feet, and bags of hand-me-downs from my cousins. I guess you can say that I've lived life at both ends of the spectrum.

I love people (most of the time). I love really getting to know people from all walks of life, especially women and girls. I love meeting women right where they are, hearing their stories, and walking alongside them to the cross to meet our Savior. I've never forgotten my own journey to find Jesus, and I want to offer this gift of knowing Him and His love for everyone.

I'm far from perfect. In fact, some days I'm basically the hot mess express, but aren't we all? If you are feeling messy or worn-out or less than, well, I wrote this book for you. I wrote it for the girls who feel like they aren't Christian enough, or good enough, or moral enough to walk into a Bible study and participate. I wrote it for all of the women who believe the lies the world has been telling us all for far too long. Those lies tell you that you aren't enough, that you aren't loveable, that you have to fit in, that you have to do certain things to please others. Those lies can damage your confidence, make you unhappy and uncertain, and keep you from the rich, close, rewarding relationship with God that you were made for.

I promise that you are enough for this Bible study. You're messy, I'm messy, we're all messy! So why not sit in the mess together and read the words that lift us all above our messes and into God's glory. Let's look at ourselves with fresh eyes, peel back the lies, and embrace God's truth and love.

> **"All Scripture is breathed out by God and profitable for teaching, for reproof, for correction, and for training in righteousness."**
> **- 2 Timothy 3:16**

What you are about to read is exactly what would take place if I were to sit down in a room with thirty to forty women. This study is a reflection on my past. It's a deep and honest look at how the Word of God has shaped my own experiences and changed my whole life.

Every time I open my Bible, I find the thread which is woven into me by the Creator. I follow that thread to His words. I tuck His words away in my heart.

When it comes to my understanding of the Bible, nothing has been cherry-picked or forced by a personal opinion. Instead, I go straight to God's Word. Then I follow the path He laid out for me, word by word, to my own understanding. I express and translate that journey to the women sitting in my Bible studies, so they, too, can rejoice in the simplicity of God's message. So that they, too, can find the thread woven inside of each of them.

His Word. My life. That's all it takes.

It gets real. There are no frills here. I am who I am, and I say it like it is. I am not here to be perfect. The Word is perfect. I am flawed. Only by showing my flaws can I reach the Word, which then helps me reach God.

That is where transformation happens.

> **"I charge you in the presence of God and of Christ Jesus, who is to judge the living and the dead, and by his appearing and his kingdom: preach the word; be ready in season and out of season; reprove, rebuke, and exhort, with complete patience and teaching. For the time is coming when people will not endure sound teaching, but having itching ears they will accumulate for themselves teachers to suit their own passions, and will turn away from listening to the truth and wander off into myths."**
> **- 2 Timothy 4:1-4**

Bible studies can be intimidating. Sitting in a room full of women you don't know to discuss the Bible? It can feel a little like going into a class and realizing there's a quiz you haven't studied for! I remember my first Bible study—I walked in and twenty minutes later, I walked out. It used to scare me when I was the new one sitting and listening. I didn't know enough. I wasn't smart enough. The Bible was just plain intimidating before I spent time reading and studying it. The leader would say, "turn to Ephesians," and I'd break into a full sweat. I didn't even know where to find Ephesians! I didn't feel worthy. In fact, I felt like an imposter! This is why Bible studies have to be in a safe place, where we can all let our guards down.

It wasn't until I let God work in my own life that the words jumped off the page.

That's when the Bible started to come alive for me. There had to be a vulnerability, humility, and the understanding that it was okay for me to be me. That's also when I realized what had been blocking me from God all along: it was *the lie*. The lie that I wasn't good enough, smart enough, or devoted enough. This is a lie that women tell themselves far too often, and one that I let define who I was for years. This study will allow you to go deeper by memorizing scripture at the end of each chapter; this will help you combat the lies that have weighed you down over the years.

See, I was adopted. The word adopted means "taken on," but all I ever thought it meant—*knew* it meant—was "left behind." Growing up, I had so many people around me who loved me, but instead of blooming in that love, I shut it out. Deep down inside, I felt like I was lost in a dark wilderness of my own.

I tended to that wilderness. I made sure it stayed locked away in my mind. I made sure nothing touched it. I didn't talk about it. I didn't pray about it. I didn't acknowledge it. I didn't admit it. And so, it grew.

Silence grows. Lies grow. The *only* way to live past a lie is to expose it. To say it out loud to a spouse, to a family member, or maybe even to a room full of women. Satan is the father of all lies. John 8:44: "You are of your father the devil, and your will is to do your father's desires. He was a murderer from the beginning, and does not stand in the truth, because there is no truth in him. When he lies, he speaks out of his own character, for he is a liar and the father of lies." What comes from God is truth and reality. What Satan gives is false! Scary, I know.

This study is broken down into six weeks in order to help you confront the lies we've all been told and that we, all too often, believe about ourselves. The lies that we aren't good enough, smart enough, or powerful enough to do God's work. Everyone hears these lies, but women, especially, face them every day.

The world is always trying to tell us what we're doing wrong. Things like ads, filters, likes, and snaps trap us in a never-ending state of comparison. Instead of looking inward to ourselves, we look outward. We compare ourselves to other people. We compare ourselves to images that have been photoshopped and filtered until they are almost unrecognizable. We compare ourselves to stories that have been edited and tweaked to promote a brand or sell a product. We start to notice only what we don't have, what we can't do, and benchmarks we haven't reached. We measure ourselves against the impossible ideals of society. It happens quietly, but the damage is unending.

I know. It took years of sitting down with my Bible to realize how many lies I told myself every day. It took even longer for me to start confronting the lies. And that work is never done. It's a constant journey.

I hope that by taking you on my journey through each and every lie, it will help you to see and challenge how each lie might be working in your own life. I really believe that the only way to take power away from these lies is to tell God, and one another, our real stuff. This makes it possible to become the people that God created us to be.

The study of the Bible is a crucial practice. And one I really believe in. Only as we accept the Bible as our supreme standard of truth can we start to live inside His spotlight.

I'm walking with you on this journey.

Love,

Shannon

Before You Begin

Before you pull out your Bible and dive in to reading and studying, I want to share a little bit about this book with you. You'll find that this Bible study won't look exactly like a lot of other Bible studies or books you may have read. It takes time to read and absorb God's Word, to think through challenging verses, to pray for God's wisdom to sink into your heart, and to talk through your findings with other women walking with you. This study spans six weeks to give you ample time for reading, study, reflection, and discussion. If you really want to read it faster—go for it! But I think you'll find the chapter-a-week pace just right for really studying these verses.

I believe that studying the Bible should be both a personal and a community activity. With that in mind, each week is broken into two sections—one meant to be read on your own and one meant to be read and discussed as a group. Since this is a Bible study after all, you'll need to have your Bible nearby to look up verses and dive a little deeper into God's Word. While I love the ease of having a verse written out in a book like this, I prefer to read the verse in my Bible. God's Word has a way of drawing me in and drawing me closer to Him. Just reading a verse without context stops you in your tracks. Reading from your Bible makes it easier for you to keep reading, to keep drawing closer with God. You should read the individual study section of each week before meeting with your group. Then read the group study sections aloud with your Bible study group and discuss the entire chapter together.

You'll see plenty of space throughout each section. This space is there for you to jot down notes, verses for further reflection, questions to discuss with the group, or prayers. It's also there to observe the Scripture. Every time you see "Let's take a moment and read," jot down any words, phrases, events, or people that jump out to you in the space provided. Watch it all come alive to you. Writing is a *huge* part of studying God's Word. So, you will also find journaling prompts throughout each chapter. You can write in the book or, if you tend to write a lot, you may want to find a pretty journal or notebook and use that for your journaling. This writing is just for you and God. Sometimes writing out answers and reviewing them later can reveal truths you may miss otherwise or topics to investigate further. Of course, you are welcome to share your answers with your group, but you certainly don't have to. You can take fifteen minutes of time during your study to journal or, if you have a more boisterous group, you can always do journaling individually after each meeting. There's no wrong way to do this—just decide as a group how to best move forward with what works for y'all!

This is the first Bible study I've ever written and it is more personal than many of the Bible studies I've participated in before. I share a lot of my heart and my story. My most sincere hope is that, by sharing the parts of me I've spent years hiding, you can find the strength to share those hidden parts of you too. It can be really scary to talk about our spiritual struggles and to admit places where we are flawed. I used to be terrified of even the idea of a Bible study. I didn't know enough. I didn't feel worthy enough. Bible studies were for the perfect women wearing pressed dresses every Sunday morning, who never had a dirty house or disobedient children. I was a mess and I did not feel like I belonged. There was so much about God and the Bible that I didn't understand. I was sure that my questions would be stupid, and everyone would be laughing at me for how much I didn't know. I was *so* wrong. So, I'm laying it all out for you here in the hopes that my struggles can inspire you to look past your ideas of what a Christian journey should look like and embrace the story God is writing just for you!

I believe in starting every Bible study by taking a good look around the room. Look at the people next to you—really look. We are all starting this journey together. Believers, non-believers, young, old—it doesn't matter. We are here.

See each other and yourself honestly. Maybe you're not in a group setting. Maybe you're doing this study in a dorm room or your living room alone. Wherever you are, *be honest*. Don't be afraid to see deep into yourself.

- What brought you here today?

- Are you scared to be here?

- Is there any part of you that feels like you shouldn't be here?

- Have you walked with Jesus for years? Or is this the very beginning of your walk with Him?

> *"Now to him who is able to do far more abundantly than all that we ask or think, according to the power at work within us, to him be glory in the church and in Christ Jesus throughout all generations, forever and ever. Amen."*
>
> *- Ephesians 3:20-21*

This verse is a central one in my life. Whenever I feel overwhelmed or insecure, I return to it. Whenever I feel like I'm in over my head, I return to it. Whenever my confidence is shaken, I return to it. It is a steady reminder that with God's power working inside of me, I am capable of so much more than I could ever possibly imagine.

I seal these words to my heart. I take another step forward.

I also urge you to consider these words as we start this Bible study. I urge you to *accept the challenge* of these words, however they may call you.

For those of you who are already on your journey with God, my challenge for you is that you allow this study to refine and reshape your beliefs. I ask you to bring whatever challenges you are facing in your life right now and see them anew through the conversation that's happening here. Challenge yourself in ways that only you and God know. What are your needs right now? Allow them to take up some space here. Allow the words to fill in your life.

For those of you who are new to Bible study, or newly on your walk with Jesus, I want this book to give you insight into who your Creator is. I want you to put any feelings of doubt and insecurity aside, with the hope that He can help you. It's OK to feel intimidated or even fearful because you know this study could reveal old hurts that have been tucked away for a long time. But remember, it could also remove the veil from your eyes and allow you to see your Creator more fully, with a love you never thought you had.

He is able to do abundantly above all that we could think or ever possibly imagine. But first, we must allow Him to.

Take this moment to say a prayer for the journey you are about to start.

WEEK ONE:
"You Are Not Enough"

"We are apt to think that everything that happens to us is to be turned into useful teachings; it is to be turned into something better than teaching . . . into character. We shall find that the spheres God brings us into are not meant to teach us something but to make us something."

- Oswald Chambers[2]

"'My grace is sufficient for you, for my power is made perfect in weakness.' Therefore I will boast all the more gladly of my weaknesses, so that the power of Christ may rest upon me."

- 2 Corinthians 12:9

Independent Study

THE BIGGEST LIE

I am going to start this study with the biggest lie of them all: *You are not enough.* This is a lie that the world tells us all the time. But it is also a lie that, much more dangerously, we tell ourselves. In moments of weakness, in moments of doubt, in moments when we have stepped out of God's light and into our own personal darkness, these are the words we whisper.

I like to picture being in God's light like it is a literal spotlight on a stage. When we are being open with God, we are standing in the center of that spotlight. When we are praying, confessing, loving one another, and serving Him, that spotlight is on us. But sometimes we turn away. We walk out of that light and try to hide within our personal wildernesses. We try doing life on our own. We slowly fade into darkness.

The lie *you are not enough* is a big part of my darkness; darkness I have faced all my life.

I was born August 25, 1971 to a mother who gave me away. The moment my life started, I was left behind. I didn't understand why. As a small child, I used to take my adoption certificate to show-and-tell at school. My friends never believed I was adopted, because I looked so much like my adoptive mom. I would often daydream, mostly during math, that my real mom was Elizabeth Taylor or Linda Carter. But then one day, I started to really wonder: "Where do my brown eyes come from? What about my singing voice? Who passed down *this* head of hair?"

I loved my parents who adopted me, and they loved me so much, but I felt different than everyone else. As time went by, that feeling of being different turned into a feeling of being *less than*. I became insecure. I started to tell myself that if my birth mother—the one person who is supposed to love you unconditionally—was willing to give me away, then I wasn't worth keeping. I was not enough.

Have you ever felt you weren't enough, or that you were less than? I'm absolutely certain you have. I still struggle with it. I work hard to be a great mom, but some days it takes every bit of energy I have just to get through the day. I hear other moms talk about their busy schedules and perfect kids—every afternoon and evening packed with extracurricular activities and sports; their volunteer work; their kids' honor roll grades, accolades, and trophies earned; and those organic, homemade meals they somehow manage to serve every night—and I know I could never keep up, even if I tried. It leaves me feeling less than. How about you?

THE BABY IN THE BASKET

Let's open to the book of Exodus. Exodus. This word means "a mass departure of people." This book marks the beginning of the departure of the Israelites from Egypt, but how did it happen? God used a baby. A small, innocent baby boy to bring forth His divine plan of greatness. That small, weak, helpless baby? He would be named Moses.

Let's take a moment and read Exodus 1:8-22.

Moses is a phenomenal but reluctant leader in the Bible, and he was born into a life that would constantly challenge his sense of belonging and his sense of worth. In this passage, his mother is preparing to send him down the Nile in a basket.

It is easy to read these words and see only the difficult obstacles that Moses faced from his very first moment on earth. Pharaoh had enslaved the Hebrew people. He had issued an order that all the Hebrew sons be taken and killed. In order to save Moses, his mother had to hide him for months. When that became impossible, she had to make the difficult choice of giving him up to be executed or placing her baby son into a basket and sending him down the river—straight into the hands of his enemies.

Every part of this seems like a bad idea. A baby? In a basket? Down a river?

Let's take a moment and read Exodus 2:1-10.

What deeply touches me about this passage is the care that Moses's mother is taking. She doesn't just use any basket. She makes this basket with her own hands using plants from the river itself. She waterproofs the basket with bitumen and pitch, so that it will be a solid vessel for this precious life. Then she puts a lid on the basket to hide the cries of the child from anyone along the river. She sends her daughter to a spot down the river where she can ensure the basket reaches Pharaoh's daughter safely. She takes every single detail into account. This passage shows her responsibility and her intuition as a mother, but it also demonstrates her trust in God.

The Hebrew word for basket used in this passage translates to "ark." An ark is a carrier of life. Water is also a symbol for life, and the water here is moving. It is physically connecting the release of the basket from the hands of one mother to the reception of the basket in the hands of another mother, Pharaoh's daughter. In a moment, when it seems that Moses's mom is risking her baby's life, she is actually handing him over *to life*.

To complete this act, there is one thing that Moses's mother needs more than anything else: faith in God. She can plan every detail as thoroughly as possible, but, in the end, she has to release the basket. She has to leave what happens next up to God. It is her child's only chance.

This highlights the extraordinary strength that is involved in the act of letting go. We all have moments when we need to let go. Oh, I know we all want to stay in control of everything as long as possible, but eventually we have to unclench our fingers and let our baskets go, to be carried away by the fast-moving waters. In order to allow God to do His work through us, we all have to let go in faith.

LETTING GO

I did not know how to let go of my insecurities about my adoption when I was standing at the edge of such a fast-flowing, treacherous river. When I entered high school, I realized no one was ever coming to look for me. The mother who had given me away was not interested in having me back. I spent many sleepless nights wondering how someone could have done such a heartless thing. Was I not the baby she wanted? Was I not cute enough? Not good enough? How could she have abandoned me so easily? I tried to have faith in God's plan for me, to let go of my wondering and trust God's love, but instead I clung even more stubbornly to my questions and fears.

Those questions took root inside my heart. They created a deep-seated insecurity that I just couldn't shake. I'd been abandoned. Instead of seeing that my parents had chosen me, had celebrated my arrival and been filled with joy to have me, I could only see that my birth mother didn't want me, didn't choose me, and had tossed me aside like I didn't matter. I felt worthless and unwanted. I felt bitter and angry. Over time, I became reckless and rebellious. It started small. For example, I wasn't allowed to listen to rock music, so I deceived my parents by recording rock and roll over my dad's sermon tapes. He'd see me on my bed with my headset on, my Bible open, as I pretended to listen to his sermons. Instead, I was listening to Bon Jovi and Def Leopard. No wonder the Bible never made sense back then—I was "Living on a Prayer" instead of actually praying! But those little rebellions quickly grew bigger. I lied about where I was going and who I was with. Those lies got bigger and bigger, as I faded into my bad choices. If my own mom didn't care about me, why should I care about myself?

WHEN WE ACT UNWORTHY

This is part of the harm that's caused by believing the lie *you are not enough*. The second we feel unworthy, we start to act unworthy.

- What, specifically, in your life makes you feel like you aren't enough?

- Has that made you act in ways that caused pain, sadness, or guilt? You're not alone in believing this lie and acting recklessly.

Let's take a moment and read Exodus 2:11-15.

In this passage, Moses is an adult. He has been raised by Pharaoh's daughter and he has been accepted by the royal family. He has wealth and power and yet he still feels like an outsider. Even though he has found a home among the Egyptians, he cannot deny or forget his Hebrew identity. This passage echoes that moment of recognition: "And he saw an Egyptian taskmaster beating a Hebrew, one of *his* people" (Exodus 2:11).

Think about the conflict Moses must have felt in this moment. Inside, Moses is both people: the Hebrew son, who was saved and nursed by his Hebrew mother, and the Egyptian son, who was adopted and raised by Pharaoh's daughter. To watch an Egyptian beat a Hebrew must have been like watching one part of himself destroy another. What a difficult thing to be faced with!

So, what does Moses do? "He looked this way and that, and seeing no one, he struck down the Egyptian and hid him in the sand" (Exodus 2:12).

He looked this way and that. He looked left. He looked right. But he took his eyes *off of God*. Moses acted on his emotions instead of looking to his Creator for guidance. By doing so, he lost himself completely. He committed a terrible sin.

This passage tells us that Moses goes out the

next day and tries to break up a fight between two Hebrews. He asks one of them why he is striking his companion, and that man answers, "Who made you a prince and a judge over us? Do you mean to kill me as you killed the Egyptian?" (Exodus 2:14).

In this moment, Moses is both identified and rejected. He realizes that even though he sees the Hebrews as his people, they don't accept him. They know him only by the crime he has committed. Pharaoh also finds out what Moses did and has no choice but to issue an order that Moses be killed, because Moses broke the law. That's a lot of rejection for one day! At that point, Moses became a man without a country. His Egyptian family has called for his death and his fellow Hebrews want nothing to do with someone who has murdered someone else.

So, Moses runs away. He flees to the land of Midian.

We humans are predictable. When we sin, there is a natural order that follows, almost every time. We feel guilt and shame. We feel unworthy of God. We may feel the need to run and hide, as Moses did. We step out of the light and into the darkness, the better to cover or camouflage our sin. Anytime we feel this yearning to hide our sins (like Moses did in the sand!), it is usually a red flag that we are on the path to darkness.

You haven't murdered any Egyptians and buried them in the sand (at least I hope you haven't!), but we don't all hide our sin so obviously. Maybe you've stopped praying. Maybe you've lied and then lied some more to cover up that lie. Maybe you've turned away from the people you love best and shut them out. Maybe you've believed so deeply that you are not good enough, that you've started to live this lie above God's truth.

BACK TO THE SPOTLIGHT

I was on that sin-hiding path in my teen years and throughout my twenties. The lies I told myself had become the foundation for my fundamental belief system. I took my eyes off of God and only saw the lies and shame I was carrying with me. The lies I'd been telling myself were so loud that nothing could drown them out. The lie that I wasn't good enough didn't go away when I got married. It didn't even go away when I had kids. I had so many amazing blessings, so many people who loved me, yet I was so caught up in my web of deceit based on my unworthiness that, deep down inside, I was sure I *didn't* deserve the good life I'd been given. I was just waiting for everyone to discover my unworthiness and abandon me like my mother had. I was anxious all the time and so very tired of carrying the weight of that lie everywhere I went.

But one day, I started praying about it. You see, my spiritual life up until this point was more of a vending machine religion than the feast that God offers each of us. I only turned to God when I was desperate. I'd pray the same way I might press F4 over and over again, hoping for a sad bag of Fritos and crossing my fingers it wouldn't get caught in the machine, just out of reach. To me, God was distant and, quite frankly, scary and intimidating. He was full of rules and the ultimate killjoy. The cop of all cops. I saw Him as fire insurance, but I was too afraid to even keep anything in the house.

Guess what brought me back into the spotlight?

A Bible study! It was there that I started to see my life through a very different lens. I started to understand the concept of prayer. In my prayers, I started asking God the questions that I had been asking myself. This opened the floodgate of praying about my adopted parents, my birth mother, and even my own family.

I prayed daily, even though it was difficult for me. At the beginning, I prayed quickly. I still wanted to hide from God, but I was trying to be brave. I knew I wasn't worthy. The ladies in my Bible study spoke of God's great love. They told me that He loved me, that He called me daughter, that He would never abandon me. The more I read the Bible and prayed, the more I started to catch glimpses of that. I was still teetering with my old way of thinking, but prayer was my lifeline at that point. It was the beginning for me. The start of something sweet and good. The fundamental building block in a true spiritual awakening. My eyes started to see God as loving and good, a Father who was for me and not against me.

Then, something very unexpected happened. In 2004, I was traveling with my husband, Phil, to NFL training camp. He was playing for the Browns that year, so we packed up our things and moved to Ohio to get ready for another football season. After we had settled in, I took my sons to watch Phil practice one afternoon. We were on the field when a stranger approached me. I was having a hard day and I wasn't in the mood to talk. But this man was patient and persistent. He kept making conversation, asking me questions. He obviously worked for the team, and I didn't want to be rude to anyone Phil worked for, so I answered his questions—short answers at first, but the more he asked, the more I opened up. By the end of the conversation, I must have told him my whole life story.

That night, Phil asked me about the conversation I'd had during his practice. The Browns employee I'd been talking to had approached Phil after we left for the day. I told Phil I might not have been as nice as I should have been, feeling a little ashamed of myself. Phil said, "Listen. He was so taken by your life story that he told me he'd like to help you find your birth family, if you want help."

I stared at Phil.

"What did you just say?" I whispered. I was shocked. Completely shocked. You see, I had been praying about this for *years*. I had begged God over and over for a deeper, more complete understanding of my past. Although my adopted parents had offered to help me find my birth parents many times, I'd always turned them down. I didn't want them to know that my deepest desire was to know more about my birth mother and to understand how she could have given me up. I didn't want them to know that inside, even though I desperately wanted these answers, I was too afraid of what the answers would be. I was afraid that any information I found would only make me feel worse and confirm that there was something inherently wrong with me—something my birth mother had seen and that that was why she'd abandoned me. I was afraid that if my birth mother found out about me, she wouldn't want to meet me and I'd be rejected by her all over again. I was afraid that even asking these questions would hurt my parents, the ones who had raised me, sacrificed for me, and loved me with a love that honestly can't be put into words.

Then one day, out of the blue, on a football practice field of all places, in a far-off city where

I had no roots and knew no one, someone who didn't even know me offered to help me? This is what people meant when they said someone was a godsend. In that moment, I felt a strange surge of freedom from my fears. I felt free enough to take a chance, to learn more. I felt free because I felt God grab my hand and lead me through a door I'd always thought was locked.

So, I trusted God and said "yes." I gave this man all the information I had about my birth, and then I waited. An entire football season passed without any answers. I started to think that maybe I'd been wrong, maybe God wasn't unlocking this door after all. Maybe this was the push I'd needed to finally come to terms with and accept that I would never know who my birth mother was or why she'd left me so long ago.

I shouldn't have doubted.

As soon as the football season was over, we loaded the kids in the car and took off for a vacation. As we were driving down a highway, my phone rang. Before I even saw his name on the screen, I knew this was the call I'd been waiting for. My heart beat faster and, with shaking hands, I answered the call.

A voice on the other end answered, "I have the information you've wanted for your entire life."

That one sentence started an unbelievable journey for me, and it left a clear divide in my life.

There is the life I've led after that call, and then there is my life before.

Before, I wandered alone in my own wilderness of lies for years. One missing piece made me feel completely broken. Back then, I could not see that everything I did up until that point was actually me hiding from God. It was me hiding inside my self-loathing, insecurity, and doubt. It was me denying my own identity as God's child, because I could not figure out whose child I was on earth. I was always afraid that if I confronted the lie *you are not enough* head on, then I would only confirm that it was actually the truth.

I know a lot of people who feel that way. They don't want to dig too deep. They don't want to question themselves or God too much. They are too afraid that the answer will be that they are not enough for this world. That they are not worth anything. That they do not have God's love. But exactly the opposite is true.

YOU ARE MORE THAN ENOUGH

We are all God's creations. God made each and every one of us. He picked each and every one of our strengths and weaknesses. To question our worth is the same thing as questioning God. When we are insecure, we are telling God that we don't have the power He gave us. We are refusing to recognize the ways He works within us. The more we reject ourselves, the more distance we put between ourselves and the Lord.

I think sometimes we are insecure because it's easier than accepting the responsibility of the power God gave us. If we believe the lie *you are not enough*, then we give ourselves permission to hide, lie, betray, and fall short. It is easier to be insecure than it is to be secure in God. Because that security takes faith.

We have all lived through difficult circumstances, some more than others for sure, but each of us can point to some event, or issue, and blame our insecurity on that. Even as I'm writing this, I know that one of my biggest struggles in life is my personal struggle with insecurity. Sometimes, I just plain think unkind thoughts about myself! I worry about what people think about me. I worry about how the things I do or say might be perceived. I worry about writing this book. I worry about hosting a Bible study. There is always the whisper inside of me that asks, "Are you really worthy enough to do this?"

I know you can relate. Haven't you asked yourself the same question? "Am I worthy enough to take on this task? Am I a good enough mom? A good enough employee? A good enough wife? A good enough friend?" We all struggle with some form of insecurity and feeling like we aren't enough.

My dad always encourages me to be a more secure leader. And he's right! Even though I can recognize the power and love in those around me, it's much harder for me to recognize those qualities in myself. I think that's a feeling a lot of people can relate to, which is why I want to point out the following truth: You are enough. You are more than enough. You are exactly and precisely what God created for this world.

God gave you the power that you have inside your heart. No matter who you are, what struggles you have faced, what sins you have committed, or what lies you might believe about yourself right now: you are valuable beyond description. You have love and strength. You have inconceivable power. You are God's child and, through Him, you can do anything.

If there is a lie blocking you from that truth, dismiss it. Remove it from the sacred chambers of your mind and heart. If there is something you need to solve, or resolve, or come to terms with in order to fully realize that truth, then pray about it. Psalms 55:22 says, "Cast your burden on the Lord, and he will sustain you; he will never permit the righteous to be moved." If you know Jesus, He will never remove your hope. Take your burdens before the Lord in prayer. If you are feeling intimidated about prayer, like I was when I first began to pray, please remember that prayer is simply having a conversation with Someone who loves you. Talk to Him like you would talk to your earthly father. Talk to Him like you would talk to your best friend over a cup of coffee. He is accessible. He is waiting for you. He is all ears when it comes to you. He always has time to listen and He honestly wants to hear everything you have to say. Nothing is off limits with Him. Prayer is a fundamental building block in the foundation of your story and in your journey.

Do not be afraid to ask questions while praying. Do not be afraid to ask for help. Do not be afraid to use the confidence God gave you. Be real, be honest, share all of your emotions. Trust me, He's God and He can handle it! Do not be afraid to say, "I am enough."

I am enough.

Group Study

✨ BIBLICAL EXCERCISE:

Let's get the ball rolling by going around the room and sharing a way (or ways) we feel that we are not enough. Do you feel like you aren't enough of a mom because you don't throw Pinterest-worthy birthday parties for your kids? Do you feel like you aren't enough of a wife because you aren't ready to leave your baby with a sitter for a date night out with your husband? Do you feel you aren't enough of a Christian, because you aren't reading your Bible every day? Or because you aren't involved in serving right now? Maybe you don't feel like enough of a friend, because you haven't called your bestie in weeks and you know she needs to talk?

You don't have to share every little detail, but I do want you to be honest about this. If you don't feel comfortable sharing with the group, that's OK, but be honest with yourself. This area (or areas!) where you feel like you are falling short? This is an area that is shrouded in lies for you. I want you to tell yourself, every day, that you are enough *with God* in this specific area. And get to praying about it! Pray for clear eyes to see the truth and lies, and pray for God to come alongside you in this specific part of your life. He's got you and He will show you the truth.

Did anyone's answer surprise you, because you thought they were more than enough in that area? Did you find yourself nodding and relating to everyone's answers?

Let's open up the conversation: for those that might know someone in the room, tell them why they are more than enough. What does she excel at that you've seen? Or what do you admire or respect about her? Maybe you don't know anyone in the room. Talk about that someone in your life, with these same qualities, to the group.

 QUESTIONS:

- What does it mean in your world that "you are not enough"?

- What draws you out of God's spotlight?

- Why is it hard to stop and prioritize God in your daily life?

- What are ways to prioritize God in your life?

- Read the text in Exodus 1:8-22. What are the things that show God working in this passage?

- Our nature is to take control. Why is that?

- Why do we fear what God could do? Why don't we allow God to work in us as he did in the midwives in Exodus 1:15-20?

- Exodus 1:19-20 is so good. See how God takes care of all the details. Fill in the blanks: The Midwives said to Pharaoh "Because the _____ women are _____ _____ the _____ women, for they are _____ and give birth _____ the midwives come to them. So _____ dealt _____ with the _____.

- How can we let God work in our more difficult situations?

- Describe a time when you were in the wilderness.

 **SCRIPTURE:**

"The Lord your God is in your midst, a mighty one who will save; he will rejoice over you with gladness; he will quiet you by his love; he will exult over you with loud singing."

- Zephaniah 3:17

JOURNAL PROMPT:

Let's start writing out your story. Identify three key points in your life: the good, the bad, and the ugly. Once that is done, take time to pray over these points and see how God might lead you to expand on these. Let me encourage you. We all have things in our lives that molded us into the people we are today. We have to start reflecting in order to see it. We have to write it down in order to release it. Remembering that God will rejoice over you with gladness.

 PRAYER:

Father, I am here. I am scared. I'm tired and I'm a mess. Please allow the time spent in this book to open my eyes and to see what You'd have me see. Open my ears to the things You would have me hear. Change my ways to Your ways through the process of stepping into Your spotlight. Begin something new in me.

I am walking with you on this journey.

Love,

Shannon

WEEK TWO:
"Don't Look Back"

"What makes authentic disciples is not visions, biblical mastery of chapters and verse, or spectacular success in the ministry, but capacity for faithfulness. Buffeted by the fickle winds of failure, battered by their own unruly emotions, and bruised by rejection and ridicule, authentic disciples may have stumbled and fallen, endured lapses and relapses . . . yet they kept coming back to Jesus. After life has lined their faces a little, many followers of Jesus come into a coherent sense of themselves for the first time. When they modestly claim, 'I am still a ragamuffin, but I'm different,' they are right. Where sin abounded, grace has more abounded."

- Brennan Manning[3]

"Let no one say when he is tempted, 'I am being tempted by God,' for God cannot be tempted with evil, and he himself tempts no one. But each person is tempted when he is lured and enticed by his own desire."

- James 1:13-14

Independent Study

MOSES IN MIDIAN

After killing the Egyptian, Moses ran away to Midian. There, he attempted to start a new life for himself. He met seven daughters of a priest at a well, and he helped them water their flock. This good deed earned him the priest's favor. Moses went on to eventually marry one of the priest's daughters, Zipporah, and she gave birth to his son.

Let's take a moment and read Exodus 2:16-22.

- Do you think Moses finds happiness here?

- What do you think are some of the inner struggles that Moses is facing in this moment?

- Why is the name that Moses gives his son so significant?

This is an eye-opening passage. Here, Moses has run away from his sin. He has not dealt with it or faced it. He has run away and hidden. That doesn't mean that what he finds in this new place is bad. It's just the opposite! Moses is welcomed in Midian. He is thriving. He is performing good deeds and receiving favor for them. It all looks perfect on the outside, but inside there is a lot that Moses hasn't resolved—his sin from Egypt, the two families he left behind, and the issues and complications of his past. <u>This is the inner wilderness that Moses gets lost in</u>.

We have all spent time lost in inner wildernesses of our own making. We have all spent years trying to outrun our heartbreak, confusion, and sin. Sometimes running away feels pretty good. A fresh start! A new you! A chance to start over! But all of that sin, and heartbreak, and confusion? There's no outrunning it. Starting over does not mean forgetting or ignoring your past.

Which brings me to the lie of this week: *Don't look back.*

This lie is often offered as advice from people we love and trust. It's offered up by society whenever things get a little too messy or destructive. It's something we tell ourselves if we have suffered a loss that seems too great or made a mistake that seems downright unforgiveable. It's a statement that is meant to give us momentum for starting over. It's meant to absolve us of the need to self-reflect, to beg for forgiveness, to seek absolution. It's meant to trick us into thinking that we don't need to tame our wilderness. We can put on a pair of stylish sunglasses, pick out a new wardrobe, and just walk away from our wilderness without a backwards glance. But the way to start over is not to erase your past self and your past experiences. You can't run away from a wilderness that lives and grows inside of you.

Do look forward. But also—do look back?

Yep, I know that might be a little confusing. Let me explain. It's OK to want a fresh start, to want to move ahead, but even if you run away, you will keep finding yourself back in the same unhappy spot (just in a different town) until you confront your own wilderness head on.

I was deep in my own wilderness in my twenties, but, despite that, my life kept moving forward in wonderful ways. From the outside, people saw a busy, happy go-getter, building a life filled with promise, never knowing that I was crying out in pain inside. In fact, some of the greatest blessings of my life happened in moments when I felt absolutely lost inside my heart. For example, I met my husband Phil when I was still struggling with questions about who I was and who I wanted to be. I wasn't in a perfect place when I met him, although I desperately wanted to be.

I met Phil backstage after a show in Arlington, Texas. I had finished a job with Wayne Newton and was now singing with the Johnnie High group—my "family," who I had performed on and off with for years. On stage with these people was my happy place. Phil had just graduated from college that very morning and was about to leave for Oakland, California to play football for the Oakland Raiders. At that point, I wasn't interested in dating. In fact, I'd sworn off men and was focused on getting right with myself. But Phil was persistent. He got my number and asked me out. We went on one date, and then he moved to Oakland. He was sweet, and kind, and different—the exact opposite of the guys I usually dated—and I couldn't help myself. I gave him a chance.

Of course, nothing about our situation was ideal for dating. I was in Texas, and he was in California. Not to age myself (yikes!), but this was before cell phones, and texting, and FaceTime. Instead, Phil and I wrote each other long, rambling letters. We spent hours on the phone—me on a landline and him on a pay phone with a bag of quarters next to him, inserting another one every few minutes just to be able to keep talking just a little while longer. We got to know each other from a distance, and somehow that made it easier to open up to him. All those hours we spent talking, pouring out our hearts to each other, we were laying a foundation that our whole marriage would be built on.

We even spent time journaling privately about our experiences and we would share those pages with one another. Up to that point in my life, I had never looked so closely at who I was and how I was created, and I hadn't done much journaling either. But, for some reason, Phil inspired me to look deeper. We were both believers, so we talked about our faith a lot. I would hang up and immediately crack my journal open; I didn't think twice about it. My ideas and thoughts basically jumped onto the page. Before I knew it, I was journaling in a way that finally pierced the chaotic wilderness I'd been wandering in.

As I wrote, I realized I'd been struggling with issues that I had never explained or even said out loud to another person. The practice of writing—taking my pain and insecurities out of the darkness and then writing them out on paper in the light—gave me such freedom and understanding. I began to understand how our minds can blur truth and make lies more believable than God's truth.

Phil and I were growing closer to each other, even though we were 2,000 miles apart. We were forming such a deep connection that it felt like we had been together forever, even though our relationship was still new. We knew God was working in our hearts for each other. I'd never really put God at the top of my list when picking a boyfriend in the past, but here I was praying about Phil and talking to him about the Bible. Phil had this definite plan for his life, with God in the center. It was new to me, but so attractive and safe. Our relationship moved quickly. I met Phil in May, we were engaged by July, and married in February. I know it sounds like a crazy whirlwind, but we'd spent so much time getting to know each other that it didn't feel that fast.

Then, a defining moment happened between us that changed everything for me.

Phil was definitely the man for me, but I didn't feel worthy of his love. I struggled so much with fear of abandonment during the early stages of our marriage. I was afraid of failure—afraid that if Phil saw me at my worst that he wouldn't want me anymore. That he might see whatever my birth mother saw in me and leave me, just like she did. That he'd see I could never measure up, and leave like all of my past boyfriends had. I thought it was impossible that someone could love me enough to really accept me—flaws and all.

Despite all of our long talks and letters and how much I loved Phil, I'd always held back emotionally because I didn't want him to see me as less than. I acted like I had everything under control and figured out. I tried to be confident, and bright, and perfect. I was a wife now, and I needed to prove that Phil had been right to choose me—messy me!—to love and marry. I wanted him to be proud of me, I wanted to be a picture-perfect NFL wife, so I stayed very busy, saying "yes" to every lunch, social commitment, event, and volunteer opportunity that came my way. I felt that if I stayed busy enough, I could focus on moving forward to prove my worth and there would be no need to look back.

Before I knew it, I had a big community of

friends and family who I saw regularly. I was doing well professionally. No one would have guessed that I was a person who didn't have it all together. No one knew about my secret wilderness. The busier I became, the less I had time to think about or even acknowledge that wilderness. Busy, social-butterfly Shannon got really good at pretending that the wilderness was gone. But it wasn't. In fact, it was still growing and expanding every day that I ignored it.

I thought I had my picture-perfect act down, but Phil saw right through me. One night during a long conversation, he said, "One day you're going to wake up and see yourself the same way that I see you." I didn't see myself as worthy, but Phil did. He saw my potential, my heart for other women who felt abandoned, and my natural leadership, even though I couldn't see any of that yet. He saw the real me—the me wandering alone in my wilderness, desperate to get out. He told me how much he loved me, and then he said the words he knew I needed to hear, "We, as a married couple, can't continue down this path in the same way that you've been walking in until now." This was it. My crossroads. My defining moment.

I knew I had to stop trying to outrun my past; I needed to turn around and face it. I needed to look back and start the process of true healing.

FACE YOUR WILDERNESS

Don't look back is a harmful lie particularly because it blocks us off. It puts up a barrier of lies between us and other people. In order to take down this barrier and live God's truth fully, we have to face the wilderness that's been growing inside of us, fed and watered by lies, and loss, and hopelessness.

We have to let others in. We must take them by the hand and guide them through the underbrush and down the dark, twisty trails forged by our pain. Tell a spouse, family member, or friend your messy truths. We all have unsaid things that we hide inside of ourselves. Maybe you've done stuff that you aren't proud of. It doesn't have to be something significant, but if it affects you negatively and doesn't align with God's Word, it can take root inside of you and grow and grow until it separates you from those you love. All too often, those secrets run so deep that they prevent us from connecting to God and to other people.

This won't be easy. And it wasn't easy for me and Phil either. We needed to dig deep into my wilderness and his, and tell each other things that were preventing us from moving forward in a healthy way. We needed to air out feelings, and issues, and old hurts that we had never discussed. Instead of breaking us, talking about those things built another layer of truth and love in our mar-

Have you ever tried to navigate this "inner wilderness" before or is it something you have avoided or not considered?

riage. For me, these truths were the core part of a past that I wanted to bury. Let's be real, it takes a lot of energy to dig up these things and place them in front of another person. It's exhausting—emotionally and physically—but it has to be done in order for healing, understanding, and closeness to bloom. I shared my deepest hurts, disappointments, pain, and personal failures with my husband. And he did the same. I felt like that day, we armored our marriage.

I didn't realize that something so personal—my own relationship with myself—could cause so much tension in the relationship I had with my husband. But the honest truth was that my past was keeping me from my future. I realized that the woman I believed myself to be was not the same woman Phil saw. He could see past the lies I was convinced were truths. He could see deeper than the pain and hopelessness I'd lived with for too long. He took me by the hand and helped me dig up and clear some of that wilderness away. He showed me that it was even possible to tame it.

Of course, that one talk didn't fix every problem we had then, but it was a start. We'd gotten married fast so we still had plenty of getting to know each other left to do. I mean, we met a lot of each other's family members for the first time at our wedding, for goodness sake! (Awkward!) Getting used to living together and figuring out how to relate to one another best and how to treat each other for the strongest marriage possible was a lot of work and adjustment. Married couples know what I'm talking about. You tie the knot and then, within a few months, you realize that there's still so much you don't know about each other.

Phil and I decided to get a third party involved to help us define and correct things that we found impossible to define and correct on our own. Let's get real: there is no such thing as a perfect marriage. We are *imperfect* people who marry each other. Marriages take work. Phil and I were willing to work, and I didn't want to start growing a new marriage-based wilderness inside of me, so we asked for help. The best phone call we ever made was to a Christian counselor.

Yes, I said counselor. Counseling is seen as a last resort for couples having *major* issues, which is a huge shame. Counseling is not a bad thing and it shouldn't be a last resort. It's a valuable tool you shouldn't hesitate to add to your marriage tool belt. Counseling does not always mean "you have a problem." You wouldn't put 6,000 miles on your vehicle and not change your oil, right? You take your car in for a tune up. Counseling can be used as a tune up for your marriage. It helps to have a Christian counselor who you can check in with, bounce ideas off of, and who can gently guide you and your spouse on the spiritual and emotional rollercoaster that is life.

We have found solid Christian counselors at different points in our marriage who have poured nothing but truth into us and have helped make our relationship stronger. It's not always pleasant. I don't want to paint a rosy picture of rainbows and butterflies here—counseling is not that most of the time. Sometimes it helps just having that third party to listen and then restate the issue in a way that helps both of us see the other's point of view. This truth telling allows you to resolve the issue and move on. Our old arguments don't resurrect themselves in that same daunting pattern of rejection, rinse, repeat. Counseling has helped us grow as a couple. Plus, we know that proactively working on our relationship sets a strong example for our kids. Phil and I both pray that our kids will see counseling as a strong tool in their arsenal, when fighting for healthy marriages in their future.

The very hardest things to talk about in marriage are the issues that you know, deep in your heart, have the potential to change everything. These truths you're afraid to share because you don't want to face rejection, are the ones you have to share in order to love and be loved fully. I thought if I showed Phil the true extent of my wilderness, he would look down on me, think less of me. I was afraid that he would think I had acted thoughtlessly and made bad decisions. I was so scared to be honest and turn a bright light on my wilderness, but I had to put my pride aside and confront the conversation with humility and honesty if I wanted to connect at the deepest level with my husband and with God.

To love God fully, you must accept yourself fully.

Deuteronomy 6:5 reminds us of this, "You shall love the Lord your God *with all of your heart*." Not just the perfect parts, without any blemishes or scars. All of your heart. And through love and understanding, you should teach those around you that it's okay for them to love with all of their hearts too. Write it on the doorposts of your house and gates. This wholehearted, full love is one of the most important ways to serve God. It is a reminder of His unconditional love for us.

PEELING BACK THE ONION

> "Am I a God at hand, declares the Lord, and not a God far away? Can a man hide himself in secret places so that I cannot see him? declares the Lord. Do I not fill heaven and earth? declares the Lord."
> - Jeremiah 23:23-24

You might be thinking to yourself right now, "How do I shine a light on my wilderness? What is there that I have not come clean about? I show my full truth to everyone. I don't have anything to hide, so I don't have anything to come clean about!"

Sorry, but I'm not buying that! Everyone has some kind of past, some kind of pain, some kind of sin that they are just burying inside themselves. Everyone has a little wilderness inside. We all have layers, like an onion. Those layers have to be peeled back in order for each one of us to fully connect to God, our spouse, family members, neighbors, and friends. As you peel back layer after layer, you'll eventually hit a layer that makes you wrinkle up your nose, because it stinks!

Yep, you do stink. I stink too. We all do. And, just like when peeling actual onions, peeling back your own layers will probably lead to a lot of tears. This is a sign that you're doing the right work.

It does no good to lock your true self away in that wilderness. When you do, you just feed the wild. That's pretty much the perfect place for sin to be born, and the perfect environment for sin to prosper. Do not give Satan an inch! Instead, open yourself up to truth and let God in.

If you are about to get married, it's a good time to peel back the onion. If you are at any kind of crossroads in your life, it's a good time to peel back the onion. This needs to happen first and foremost with the Lord. Then with a spouse. Then with family and friends.

I can tell you that once you start taming the

wilderness and peeling back the onion, you will be met with incredible, freeing grace. Not only from God Himself, but from the people you love who fully accept you. Once you shine a light on your truest, most honest, messy self, you can love the Lord God with your big, wide-open heart. And that is where real healing begins.

THE POWER OF THE PAST

The most difficult times in our life change us. If we never look back, we might forget just how far we've come. Those difficult times are powerful reminders of growth and humility. The pain we've experienced during challenging moments can serve as markers along our life path. When we start to go off track, those markers show us how we regained our footing before. When we find ourselves at a crossroads, those markers can show us which path to take and remind us that we've risen above bad situations in the past, and that we can do it once more. When we've known pain and sin intimately, we never want to feel it again. Remembering the past helps keep us from repeating the same mistakes over and over again. The past gives you a well of knowledge that you can pull from in times of hardship. Difficult times also serve to remind you of God's unending mercy and forgiveness.

> Your story is powerful. Its a gift. No matter how messy or simple it is, It can be used for his glory!

Look at your life as a shadow box. Place the things that remind you of where you've been in the bottom row of your box. Then place the things that God has blessed you with on the top row. One row is not more important than the other. Both rows represent redemption and grace.

Let's take a moment and read Romans 8:1-11.

This passage is a good reminder that living honestly means living in the Spirit. There is no condemnation for those who are in Jesus Christ. God knows we sin. God knows we are not perfect. He sees us during the most difficult, dark, and pivotal moments in life, and He is there. He will never leave us. He has been patiently waiting for us to return to Him.

The fact that God is there even in our worst moments is proof that we serve a loving, gracious, and sovereign God, who cares for us beyond what we can imagine. It's through life's detours, pitstops, and wrong turns that we truly realize the power of God's forgiveness and grace. You can say to yourself, "God loved me so much that I'm here today, strong enough to even be able to express and talk about it." The fact that we are all here today is because, at some crossroads in our life, we picked the path that led to Him.

Your past does not define who you are, but

understanding it helps you better understand the person you have become. It will also help show you the way forward. When you have an understanding of who God is, and how He loves you, and why He created you, you can move freely in the direction in which He wants you to go. I think a lot of people get bogged down with this idea that God is this judge and dictator up there, who could smite you at any moment. But that's not who He is. He's full of love, mercy, and grace. He is a just, but loving God.

Let's take a moment and read Exodus 2:23-25.

We return to Moses. He has been in Midian. He has been moving forward with his life in a place far from his home. But there are things happening at home that he won't be able to ignore. The slaves of Israel are in pain and they are crying out for help. They need someone to come free them. God hears them, and what does God do?

God remembers his covenant with Abraham, Isaac, and Jacob. He sees the people of Israel and <u>*He knows*. He knows they have to be saved</u>. He knows someone who can do it, someone who has been promised to do it. He knows what Moses is capable of.

God does not abandon Moses because Moses abandoned Egypt. God does not punish Moses for running away. God simply seeks Moses out and encourages Moses to live God's purpose for his life. God is always waiting for us to come back to Him. God has a much bigger purpose for each of us than we could ever possibly see or imagine.

It is difficult to see or trust that we are meant for something much bigger than our immediate lives. It is hard to accept the fact that our past does not define us. Moses is a perfect example of a leader who did not always trust himself or his abilities. He had as many doubts and insecurities as anyone else. He was someone who knew he could do wrong, that he could sin, that he might make the wrong decision in an important moment. He was full of uncertainty. But God called him anyway. God used Moses's past, used Moses's internal wilderness, and used Moses's faith to lead His chosen people out of slavery in Egypt. If God can redeem Moses's past, He can redeem yours too.

As this week ends, I urge you to think about how your past can make you stronger today. Think about the lessons you have learned that you have carried with you. Let go of some of the lies that you've been telling yourself. Let go of your insecurities and doubts. Let go of the blame that you have directed at yourself for past events. Accept that God has a much bigger plan for you than you could ever know. Redirect and refocus on God's plan for you. Rest, relax, and lean into His purpose for you, accepting that He is in control.

Look back and see what treasures you find.

Group Study

✦ BIBLE STUDY EXERCISE:

Let's go around the room (for those that are comfortable) and share one fact about our lives that we aren't so proud of. It doesn't have to be anything big. It can be something really small. Or it can be something significant that has been burdening you for a long time. Say whatever you want to get out right at this moment. The point of this exercise is to practice honesty, understanding, and acceptance. Please know this: transparency is almost impossible to achieve, but honesty is very obtainable. If you can't bring yourself to share with the group, that's OK. But get brave and at least be honest with your Heavenly Father. Go to Him and pray. Tell Him about your wilderness, peel back your onion for Him, and let His grace be your resting place. You're on the road to burning away the lies that have grown in your mind. You are replacing them with the redeeming love of a God who is fully accepting of you!

What is one thing that has shaped you into who you are today and why?

- What can we learn from this exercise?

- Did the truths in this room surprise you?

- How do you think living more honestly in your day-to-day life can help you, and others, grow in God's love?

*looking back is important - its kind of like when you are hiking a mountain. Its important to give yourself a break and look back at the view and what you climbed. Be **proud** of that!*

QUESTIONS:

- Which do you do more: reflect/look back or avoid/look ahead? Why?

   both? i feel like its rly hard for me to be in the present

- What unresolved issue from your past are you most aggressively trying to avoid today?

- Is it possible that trusting in our loving God to comfort, console, and correct us while "looking back" will produce spiritual growth and intimacy with Him?

- To understand a well-written book, one must finish each chapter before moving on to start reading the next. What chapters of your life have you not finished "reading"?

- Who do you think is most pleased when you live in shame, regret, and embarrassment? God or Satan?

  Satan! God has a gift waiting for us (grace) that he is just waiting for us to accept.

- Who do you think offers forgiveness, freedom, and purpose? God or Satan?

  God - but we have to embrace that.

- Why do we cover up our stuff with the business of life? Are you guilty of this?

> So i can avoid my feelings. I notice I have worked more when i am unhealthy.
>
> also so I can build myself up. When I feel bad about myself I do this.

- Why is it hard to start our process of "peeling back our onion?"

> i hate being the first one to do it! It's scary. Its also hard to bring up. I also think it can be scary to think that those ~secrets~ can turn into gossip/rumors

- Can you clearly define God's grace in your life? Explain.

Does your relationship with God look intimate?

- Do you truly understand that God desires a relationship with you no matter your past, no matter how far you are from Him? How do you have a personal relationship with Him?

SCRIPTURE:

"Have I not commanded you? Be strong and courageous. Do not be frightened, and do not be dismayed, for the Lord your God is with you wherever you go."

- Joshua 1:9

✏️ JOURNAL PROMPT:

Let's read Isaiah 43:1, "Fear not, for I have redeemed you; I have called you by your name, you are mine." Let these words really sink in. Let's pick up in your own story with writing about the process of peeling back the layers of your onion to give you a clear and honest look into your past. Acknowledge where you came from and where you are today. Write with honesty and conviction. Remember, there are no secrets hidden from God. Be strong and courageous, and write!

What has shaped you into who you are today?

 **PRAYER:**

God, we stand before You as broken people. We might look as if we have it all together, but we are hurting inside. As the author of our story, as the God of our life, take our mess. Heal us from the inside out. Give us the strength to look back on where we came from, but with an understanding of Your grace, Your unmerited favor poured out on our lives. Allow us to trust in You and to trust that where we are going is by Your design. Let us lean into You from here on out.

I am walking with you on this journey.

Love,

Shannon

WEEK THREE:
"You Need It"

"Ultimately, God isn't good because he does good things for us. And God isn't good because of something in us. God is good because of something in him. He can be nothing else. Both God and his choices remain good, even when they may not feel or look particularly good to you. His intrinsic eternal nature, in all of his attributes, is good."

- Chip Ingram

"I am the vine; you are the branches. Whoever abides in me and I in him, he it is that bears much fruit, for apart from me you can do nothing."

- John 15:5

Independent Study

ESTHER BECOMES LEADER AND QUEEN

There is so much pressure from the outside world that sometimes, as women, we lose ourselves quietly to the demands nipping at our heals daily. The news, talk shows, magazines, and social media all compete to set the bar for our success, and I feel like I'm constantly trying to extinguish those ideas. This week's lie is going to focus on that pressure. The IT that we feel like we MUST DO in order to be good wives, moms, friends, and neighbors. The IT is different for everyone. Your IT could be owning a new house or a new car. The IT could be making sure your kids play every sport or get into the best schools. The IT could be finding the trendiest vacation spot or serving on every board. The point is that whatever IT is, <u>you are being told by everyone else that IT will make your life more meaningful and you more important, or happy, or fulfilled</u>.

The problem with this lie is that you can change everything around you one hundred times over and IT will not make a difference. True change, true strength, and true value all happen on the inside. So, this week's Bible study highlights a figure who knew that her value and worth came from the inside and that her real power came from being God's loving and humble servant. This week's study focuses on Esther.

Let's take a moment and read Esther 2:1-18.

Esther's father and mother are dead. She has been adopted and brought up by her uncle, Mordecai. He took her in, raised her, and protected her. He is the only father figure she has, and she trusts in him, believes him, and loves him as if he were her real father. It's a beautiful thing to see the relationship described between Esther and Mordecai in this passage.

What's also interesting about this passage is that the first two chapters of Esther place a lot of emphasis on beauty. Queen Vashti is noted as being beautiful, and she is punished for not showing her beauty to the court at the king's request. This prompts the king to throw what basically resembles a modern-day beauty pageant to help him choose a queen to replace Vashti. Specific beauty rituals are mentioned here. Cosmetics. Ointments. Six months with oil of myrrh and six months with spices and ointments—*things* meant to enhance the beauty of the women who are competing for the title of queen.

Esther wins favor quickly. How does she do this? By her actions. If you pay attention to the passage, it tells us that Esther is beautiful at the beginning of her story. Yet every time she wins favor, it is because of her behavior. She wins the favor of Hegai by her pleasing manner. She remains obedient to Mordecai by not revealing her Jewish identity as he requested. When she goes into the court and is allowed to take whatever she desires, she asks for nothing except what Hegai advises. She is not greedy. She does not try to overextend her power. And so, the passage says, she wins favor in the eyes of all who see her.

This is a good reminder that true beauty lies within us. It is God's grace radiating from us. It is a peace we can also extend to others and a quiet power given to us by the Lord. Can you remember a time when you decided *not* to believe the lie *you must do IT* and instead focused on the worth inside yourself?

I DIDN'T NEED IT

When I married Phil, I also felt like I married the NFL. His job as a professional kicker was more than a job, it was a lifestyle for both of us. Walking into my NFL life was a little (OK a lot!) intimidating. I had no idea what I was in for!

Since Phil and I dated long distance, I didn't really experience the world of the NFL until after we got married, and it wasn't like I had the chance to wade in slowly—I got thrown right into the deep end. A few months after we got married, Phil and I packed the car and drove to Ohio together for training camp. I unpacked the car that same evening, while Phil went to a meeting. He was gone for hours. I was left in an apartment by myself in a city where I didn't know anyone. I felt really trapped and isolated in that moment. I remember thinking to myself, as I looked around our sad, empty apartment, *what have I gotten myself into?* I needed to be busy. I needed to have my world, my job, and my community. I needed to go places, see people, and do things. I felt paralyzed, because I was so out of my element. To make matters worse, we only had one car, and Phil needed it to drive to and from practice and meetings. I was stuck by myself.

Once Phil checked into camp, I was able to go up there and see him in fleeting moments. Thirty minutes here. Thirty minutes there. I often say football players meet more often than the Baptists! To this day, twenty years later, I'm still not sure what they meet about for all of that time. When Phil mentioned that we would be going to dinners with players and coaches, I brushed up on the rules of football. I was the cheerleader in high school who cheered for offense when our team was playing defense, so, believe me, it was an uphill climb! During that process, I read a lot of articles about the team. I worked to learn who the players were and if they were married or had girlfriends. I was actively seeking a community of women. I wanted to find my people. I remember meeting the spouses and families at training camp and thinking, *We're all in the same boat. Let's do this together.*

Don't get me wrong, the people were amazing. But the NFL itself, that was really strange to me. There were a lot of appearances to be made. There was a lot of power and money floating around. It was not at all a world I was used to. And suddenly, it was *my* world. Phil and I were invited to parties, events, and dinners. I felt a lot of pressure to measure up and to be a wife who supported my husband and represented him well. That pressure grew louder and louder, until I was consumed with all of the ITs I needed to do to keep up.

I'm sure you've been there. Maybe not the NFL part, but there have been times when your social calendar could rival the best of them, right? Admit it, you feel accomplished at saying "YES!" to everything. You're the one everyone counts on. The life of the party. In all the pictures and getting all the likes. Each "yes" leads to more friends and more events. Before you know it, every night of the week is filled with stuff. And that's just the nights! It then rapidly rolls over to your days. Do I need to say more?

Luckily, it didn't take me long to see this lie for what it was. I didn't need "IT," I only needed Him. There were all these unwritten rules, but I remember making a decision to ignore rules and do this differently. I was not going to play by the world's rules or the NFL's. Instead, I chose to play by the rules I knew to be true and reliable, and I'm still playing by those rules. I didn't need "IT" to be something I wasn't. I didn't need "IT" to make me feel a certain way. I'm me, the one God created, hard-wired just how He wanted me, and I'm proud of it. I rocked an outfit from Target at one of our first events; I wore it like Sandra Bullock wore her Louis Vuitton dress at the Oscars. Own who you are and Whose you are, ladies. Allow your beauty to come from within you.

Esther embodies that. To me, Esther is a woman of grace. She is a person who follows God wholeheartedly and finds her ultimate fulfillment in Him. The entire story of Esther illustrates God's great plan unfolding despite the world's challenges.

Let's take a moment and read Esther 2:19-23.

We find a good example of the divine plan that weaves in and out of this scripture at the end of Chapter 2. Here, Mordecai discovers a sinister plot. The text tells us that Mordecai was always around the king's gate. That means that Mordecai had some kind of official position in Xerxes judicial system, because judges sat at the gate in these times, and that would've helped Mordecai to hear about the guards' plot to kill the king.

This position helped Mordecai keep an eye on Esther. He had let her go in, but he was still being a protective father. He made sure she didn't disclose that she was a Jew, because he knew it would be harmful for her. He also knew she was going to do great things in there. So, the relationship between Esther and Mordecai remained strong, even after she enters the court. When Mordecai overhears a plot to kill the king, he reports it straight to Esther who passes it on to the king's men. The report is investigated and found out to be true. The guilty men are punished, and then it is recorded in the book of the Chronicles that Mordecai saved the king. This is a really important point that ties straight to God's plan!

I want to pause here a moment and emphasize that idea of God's plan. As individuals, we tend to focus only on ourselves. We have moments when we struggle to connect to other people, to feel what they are feeling, and to see the world from a larger point of view. We mostly only see the world from the viewpoint of our personal window, or our little box of reality. But it's important that we don't stay there, that we realize what we're seeing is a very small picture. Look outside your box and understand that God is there, seeing the bigger picture. He's got this. Learn how to trust Him when you can't see everything. When you aren't told everything. Don't allow your own narrow point of view to limit your trust in Him.

- Has there been a moment when you struggled to see the bigger picture in your life?

- What happened that made you come back to God and His vision for your life?

One character in Esther's story who illustrates this tunnel vision is Haman. Haman has a big ego problem and it's only getting bigger.

Let's take a moment and read Esther 3:1-15.

The passage opens with a promotion for Haman and the king's order that everyone at the gate must bow down to Haman in his new position. There is one person who doesn't bow down to Haman and that's Mordecai. Why is this? It could've been merely pride. Mordecai is a Jew and he makes an issue out of the fact that Jews don't bow down to people.

So here, Haman has taken on this new position of power, but he is using it the wrong way. He is using it for bad instead of good. He goes so far as to bring this request to the king, and how does he phrase it?

Scripture tells us in Esther 3:8 that Haman said to the king, "There is a certain people scattered abroad and dispersed among the peoples in all the provinces of your kingdom. Their laws are different from those of every other people, and they do not keep the king's laws, so that it is not to the king's profit to tolerate them." Because the Jews were God's people and living according to His principles, Haman detested them. In this little moment of revenge, he has no problem extending his loathing of one person, Mordecai, to an entire group of people. This is a real signifier of someone who is harboring hate inside of his heart.

The last line of this passage tells us that the city is thrown into a state of confusion because of Haman's action. There is one person especially who has been forced into a full-blown wind of confusion, and that's Esther. As if keeping her heritage a secret wasn't difficult enough when the stakes were lower, now she could be killed if she reveals herself as a Jew. Think about what it must have taken to hold a position like hers, so high up in the king's court, and have a secret that big. Does she just have so much grace and courage that it's easy for her? No, definitely not.

Let's take a moment and read Esther 4:1-11.

Here we really see Esther's doubt. She's a human, just like everyone else. She's afraid, unsure, and filled with insecurity. When Mordecai sends a message through the gate asking Esther to plead with the king on behalf of her people, Esther responds by basically saying that she hasn't been called to go to the king. She knows that the price of going to the inner court of the king without being called upon is death unless the king holds out his golden scepter. And what we can see flash through Esther's mind here is A) "They don't know I'm a Jew. What's going to happen when they find out I'm a Jew?" and B) "Even though the king has shown me favor and is taken with my beauty, I don't know if that is going to be enough to save me." Esther is terrified.

But Mordecai's response is perfect. He says,

"Do not think to yourself that in the king's palace you will escape any more than all the other Jews. For if you keep silent at this time, relief and deliverance will rise for the Jews from another place, but you and your father's house will perish. And who knows whether you have not come to the kingdom for such a time as this?" (Esther 4:12).

Let's read his full response in Esther 4:12-17.

Mordecai is reminding Esther of her place in the world here. He is making the window through which she sees the world a little bit bigger. He is basically saying: "Remember who you are. Remember that you are part of a bigger people. Remember that you are part of a family. Do not think that you can escape alone. Silence will not free you. You are part of this because you exist. You are part of a greater vision: God's vision. And that will take place whether you decide to participate or not."

Esther hears Mordecai. She answers by obeying him. She also extends that obedience to God. Her action here is fasting. She has Mordecai and his people fast as well. And she says in her message to Mordecai, "I and my young women will fast as you do."

A COMMUNITY OF WOMEN

Not only has Esther has just acted in obedience, she has also revealed herself as a leader. This is much bigger than her title of queen. Someone can have that title, which is an earthly title, without getting any of the respect or power attached to it. But being a leader means inspiring loyalty in the people around you. Esther is a leader, not just a queen. She does not say, "I will fast." She says, "I and my young women will fast." When I read this passage, I think to myself, *she must be someone who treats the people around her with fairness, generosity, and respect*. This is why they are so blindly loyal to her, following her with the same faith with which she follows God.

As women, it's important to have the support of a community of women. You need to find your people, a group of friends, a Bible study, a mom crew. These groups provide a safe place for women to find advice, accountability, growth, and community, which are hopefully all led and inspired by God's Word. We had an incredible Bible study leader in Ohio, while Phil played for the Cleveland Browns. The group leader, Joann, provided a place where we could bring our questions and concerns. We could discuss our thoughts and grow in the knowledge of the Lord. We all came from different backgrounds. We were all different ages. We were all from different ethnicities. The diversity added this layer of depth to our group that was truly so insightful and beautiful. The wider variety of perspectives made discussions more meaningful.

THE COUNSEL OF THE WISE WOMAN

"She opens her mouth with wisdom, and the teaching of kindness is on her tongue."
- Proverbs 31:26

We must seek counsel from other women, especially women who are in different seasons of life. There is wisdom in every season, but it's not always easy to recognize that. For example, in my twenties, I viewed myself as a grown up. I didn't ask for help much. I was a working professional who had (somewhat) arrived with all the answers—or so I thought! I, for sure, was doing IT to please others.

I see young women who feel this way all the time! It's an important life stage. The independence is exhilarating. But it is a mistake, at any point in life, to stop seeking counsel. At twenty, we feel this invincibility and this entitlement of "I am finally here." We are in a car driving full speed ahead to bright and happy futures, at least until something inevitably goes wrong.

The book of Proverbs makes it clear that older women have wisdom. I think that's something, as a culture, that we have lost sight of. Now, we don't necessarily have to go to every elderly woman that we see and say, "Teach me!" That is a good thing to do, but seeking counsel from a wise woman doesn't need to be that stereotypical and obvious.

In your twenties, there is a thirty-year-old who has lived life right ahead of you and has experience and exposure to share with you that can really enlighten your next ten years. If you're thirty, there's a forty-year-old. And so on. Seek out these ladies. Make them a part of your life, your groups, your Bible studies. You will get wise counsel that will help you navigate through this messed up world.

Often in life, we sell ourselves short by not taking advantage of the opportunities that are right around us. Choose your friends wisely. Hang out with those that will be honest and talk to you about the hard stuff. Find friends that lift you up. Not friends that fill you full of, "You must do IT in order to . . ." fill in the blank. Finding friends of different ages is very important. That's what I have done with my circle of friends and it has been such a blessing. For example, one of my dearest friends, Stephanie, is seven years younger than me. Another one of my dearest friends, Linda, is eighteen years older than me. My longtime friend, Katie, is my age. It creates this valuable spectrum of experience and insight. I value all of their opinions, and it's funny how each one of them speaks to me differently.

I hear it all the time in Bible study: Ladies don't want to admit weakness or lack of intelligence. We want to be seen as having it all together and figured out. Those who can seek the right friends of all ages are the ones who get their cup filled with goodness, wisdom, strength, encouragement, honesty, confidence, and unconditional love. They, in return, become great examples and leaders for the ones around them.

Esther is this kind of leader. She does not tell Mordecai that she knows better. She does not ignore his plea. She does not even go the path alone. She turns to the women around her and fasts with them.

There's no strength in going it alone. By showing your vulnerability to someone else, you are grabbing an opportunity to grow. Listening to others and learning from them can help you move past the problems you might sometimes get stuck in. Asking for help gives you a way forward. And that's what God calls us to do. He calls us to keep moving forward in our faith, so that we do not get stuck in stagnant water.

If there is no movement in your faith, it's time to check in with yourself and the people around you. You can move toward God through prayer, studying His Word, worship, your thoughts, and your decision making. There should be this thread of Jesus in everything you do. And that thread should be extended to those around you. Find your women. Move forward together in the Lord's name.

ESTHER GOES TO THE KING

We left Esther in a state of insecurity. In her mind, she isn't sure if she can do what Mordecai is asking of her. It's a human response. Then the reality of the situation sets in, and she remembers that she is a child of God. She is a Jew. So, she decides with boldness that she is going to do what is asked of her. As frightened as she is, she knows that her feelings are not going to decide this for her. She knows she is meant to take action for God no matter how she feels. She knows what is at stake—approaching the king without an invitation could mean death. Esther says in chapter 4:16, "I will go to the king, though it is against the law, and if I perish, I perish." She prepares for her meeting. Take note of the order here: she prays, fasts, and relies on the community around her, then everyone follows her. Wow, could you do this? This is a great way to see where your heart for the Lord is. Could you stand up for God and take action even if it meant death?

Let's re-read Mordecai's statement in chapter 4:13-14.

In this statement, there is a point being made that, for me, was like a shot in the arm. The point that, if Esther isn't going to do it, then God will find someone else to do it. For us, this means God wants to use us like he used Esther—in our homes, Bible studies, offices, schools, and communities.

That's a real key point here. We are not on this earth to be passive. We are meant to take action for God. Regardless of the way it feels in the moment, it is our calling to step up to any kind of challenge that falls across the path of life. You have the right and the responsibility to step up in a bold manner. If you don't do it, it's going to come from someone else. God will do what He will do, period. Are you up for the challenge?

I was scared to death when I got the phone call that suggested I should write this book. I laughed out loud, saying, "You do know I almost failed English, right?" I'm not qualified to write. The publisher heard my doubt and reminded me that God uses ordinary, messed up people, like me, to do His work. After much prayer, counsel, and discussions with my husband, we decided there's no perfect time or season for something like this. Spoiler alert: there never will be! It will always be hectic. So, I wrote, knowing that if God put this on my radar, and I've had nothing but green lights and silent nudges from Him, then I needed to write.

God sees the bigger picture much more than I could ever see. Trusting that He will grow me through the writing process or possibly inspire a future reader's heart for the first time. We can be fed our entire life through church, Bible studies, and friendships, but if we don't take what we've learned and apply it, what are we doing but just taking in life?

The application part is just as important as the absorption part. Both are a *must* in your walk with the Lord. When you absorb God's Word and His truth along with life experiences, you're establishing layers of knowledge and growth in your heart. Then you can apply those truths to your everyday existence. In return, you can rest in the quiet confidence that can only come from the Lord. When we learn about God and then apply it to our life, allowing faith to anchor us, we have an opportunity to see Him more clearly. John 20:31 says that the things written in the Bible are written so that we can believe Jesus Christ the Son of God, and that, by believing, we may have life in His name. We must recognize the lie, but then reject it, replacing it with truth.

I've heard it said that it would be better to be considered a failure than to be counted as disobedient. Just like Mordecai said, "If you don't do it, God will find someone who will." Have you ever been afraid to step out of what's comfortable and trust big?

Even though Esther is afraid of talking to the king, she goes to him. She does not know the full circumstances. She does not know what the outcome will be. She knows she might be killed if the king does not agree with her. She really doesn't have a foot to stand on. As a result, she has to truly depend on God to carry her through. That is such a beautiful picture of what faith is.

- Where do you doubt God in your life?

- Now, choose one of those doubts and write about how you can allow your faith in God to help you let go of this.

Let's take a moment and read Esther 5:1-8.

I picture Esther in this passage as a radiant statue. It said earlier in the text that she was beautiful. I see her standing before the king, wrapped in just her beauty and certain grace. She has prepared herself for this moment. The passage does not name the more superficial ways she prepared for meeting the king (unlike in the passage earlier, when it specifically mentioned that all the women who were appearing before the king were using spices and ointments). We only know that to meet with the king, Esther prepared by fasting and praying. She found strength in God. And that is what is allowing her to stand strong before the king as she makes her request.

As we close this week of study, this is the image I want to end with. I want us to think about Esther wrapped inside her strength, faith, and duty. I want us to imagine her standing in virtue before the king. She does not need IT, she does not need anything in this moment, except her own courage, grace, and faith in the Lord.

Likewise, you do not need anything but God on your journey to the cross.

You don't need anything but God.

Group Study

"Blessed is everyone who fears the Lord, who walks in his ways."
- Psalms 128:1

 **BIBLICAL EXERCISE:**

Take a few minutes to discuss all of the "ITs" we think we need to be happier or more fulfilled. What is the thing you see on friend's social media accounts that makes you feel jealous or like a total failure because you don't have IT? Is IT an impeccably decorated home that never seems to get dirty? Is IT date nights at all the coolest restaurants? Is IT time and a gym membership to exercise every day and shed those last few pounds of baby weight? From our study this week, we know that the only thing we actually need is God, so why do these things keep haunting us? Discuss with the group why you can't seem to let go of thinking your IT will change your life.

What does your IT represent to you really? Do you want to lose weight to feel beautiful? Do you want the perfect date nights, because you are scared you are drifting apart from your husband?

- What are some other ways you can address those ITs? Prayer, of course, but what else?

 **QUESTIONS:**

- What are three lies you have struggled with? Write them out here. I must do/have IT in order to . . .

- Give 3 reasons why you believe those lies:

- What internal or external factors drive your decision making?

- Whose approval do you find yourself most trying to earn?

- Knowing what you have learned in this chapter, how could you have handled things differently?

- Where are you seeking most of your counsel from? The world's view, books, friends, the Internet, or God's Word? Why? (Be honest with yourself.)

- Could you take a stand for Christ no matter the cost? Write about what it would look and feel like to boldly stand.

- Jesus promised us in John 14:6, "I am the way, and the truth, and the life . . ." How should that affect your worldview?

- Can you name one thing that you absorbed from this chapter that demands a change in you?

- How can you apply that today?

 **SCRIPTURE:**

"She is clothed with strength and dignity, and she laughs without fear of the future."

- Proverbs 31:25 (NLT)

JOURNAL PROMPT:

I want us to take a closer look at the principle of application in our walk with the Lord. As much as it is important to hear God's Word, it's even more important to *apply* His Word. How do you do that? I like to look at it like this:

PSM—where P is personal, S is specific, and M is measurable.

- P = This personally applies to me.
- S = How, specifically, do I need to change?
- M = How can I measure how much I've changed?

How can this system be used for the chapter we just read? Let's say you struggle with fear and doubting, like Esther. Then:

- I know I have fears. What are they? (That's the personal.)
- I need to look for ways to handle my fears. (That's the specific.)
- I'm going to check back with myself in one week to see how I handled my fears. (That's the measurable.)

For your journal this week, write your entry using this PSM system. As you reflect on this chapter, think about what you are struggling with. How are you going to allow God's Word to sink in and be applied to your life?

Before you write, read and reflect on 2 Timothy 1:7: "For God gave us a spirit not of fear but of power and love and self-control." Allow these words to marinate. Write what they mean to you. Pray and ask God to reveal your inner struggle. Once again, peel back your layers and find the one that needs attention. Allow that struggle to pour out of you onto this paper. Ask for change in yourself—that you will see yourself as fearfully and wonderfully made to stand boldly in Christ Jesus. You can't be your true self if you're not honest with yourself. God created you to be something special. He didn't create you to be boring or unworthy or like any other person. Stand boldly for Him. Continue to peel back the layers. It will be so worth it.

 **PRAYER:**

Father, we are excited to meet with You today, opening our hearts to new and wonderful things. Show us the things You desire for us to change. Allow us to start to break down any misconceptions we've harbored over Your desire for our lives, as we hit an all-too-familiar lie today. Prepare us as we absorb Your Word and then apply it to our life.

I'm walking with you on this journey.

Love,

Shannon

WEEK FOUR:
"You Have to Fit In"

"The remarkable thing about fearing God is that when you fear God you fear nothing else, whereas if you do not fear God you fear everything else. Blessed is every one that fears the Lord."

- Oswald Chambers[6]

"Beloved, do not be surprised at the fiery trial when it comes upon you to test you, as though something strange were happening to you. But rejoice insofar as you share Christ's sufferings, that you may also rejoice and be glad when his glory is revealed."

- 1 Peter 4:12-13

Independent Study

STAKE YOUR CLAIM

This week, we're going to continue with our study of Esther. I believe there is so much to learn from her and her quiet nature. Esther is a person who knew how to stand her ground. She did not follow the crowd. But she also did not make a show of being different, or take any pride in standing out. Instead, she just quietly followed the path that God laid out for her with absolute conviction and with faith in Him above all else. She did not look to other people for acceptance. She knew the only acceptance that mattered was His.

Which brings me to the lie of this week: *You have to fit in.*

It is a completely normal feeling to want to belong. We all want to be accepted and loved. There's nothing wrong or weird about that. After all, we were made to live in community. But it is important to know when to follow the crowd and when to go a different direction. It is important to have the conviction of your faith, so you can hear God's voice nudging you in the right direction above all others. To follow God, we often have to leave the crowd behind and forge our own path.

Let's take a moment and read Esther 5:1-8.

This passage opens with Esther going to the inner court of the king's palace. Esther is certainly not being timid here. She knows this action can get her killed if the king does not show favor to her, but she stands in front of the king's quarters anyway.

I envision this scene with Esther, dressed in her royal robes, standing as still as a statue in front of the king, who sits on his throne. In my mind, she looks radiant, calm, and gorgeous. She's not hooting and hollering. She's not making a scene. She's bold, but at peace. When the king sees this, he extends his golden scepter to her. He recognizes her calm demeanor and purpose, so he allows her to step forward. Then he asks her, "What is it, Queen Esther? What is your request? It shall be given you, even to the half of my kingdom." (Esther 5:3).

Now, we know from the beginning of this book that this king is not one to give things to people who do not deserve them. Remember Queen Vashti? He took away her title for disobeying him. So, it's not that this king is a generous and giving leader. It's that there is confidence radiating from Esther, something that commands the attention of the entire room and earns the king's respect. So much so, that he offers half his kingdom to her before she even asks for one single favor.

I really think, as women, we all need to hold on to this image of Esther. She is standing tall and confident. She is calm and quiet. She does not have the loud and in-your-face persona that we are so used to seeing in our own society. Instead, she is regal. She is quietly, but powerfully, staking her claim. Be careful not to read Esther's calm as passiveness or embarrassment. No, Esther is boldly standing for the truth.

Can you think of a moment when you had to stake your claim and stand up for something you believed in?

THE SEVEN MILE MOVE

For me, one of the moments that most stands out in my journey is something that I'm going to call the Seven Mile Move. It happened when Phil and I were living in Austin, Texas. When we first moved there, we rented a house to study churches, neighborhoods, and schools. We found a house in the perfect neighborhood for our needs at the time. With much prayer and thought, it felt right to go from renting to owning. I started leading Bible studies in our new community. The number of people coming to Bible studies every week climbed and climbed. It became normal for a room to fill up on a Thursday.

Of course, it wasn't just me leading. I've always been blessed to have really good wingmen to co-lead with me. Just like Goose was crucial to Maverick in *Top Gun*, or Chewbacca was to Han Solo in *Star Wars*, as a leader you'll need a wingman to be an extra set of eyes and ears in the room, to jump in and contribute to discussion, to lead in times when you need to step away, or just to have a prayer partner. It's hard to go at this alone. So, thanks to my many wingmen over the years: Stephanie, Amber, Holly, Kerri, and Libby.

The whole neighborhood Bible study thing threw me into a central role in that new community. I wasn't just seeing people every week at home. I was running into friends in the grocery store, at school, in between carpooling, everywhere. It got to the point where I planned in extra time for my grocery and Target runs. I knew I'd end up talking over the avocados or in the frozen food aisle, hearing the needs of others or encouraging them to continue to give Bible study a chance. God really intertwined my life with the lives of the people around me. It was a wonderful blessing and a really beautiful time in our lives. All these people who had deep roots in this community had accepted us, and we felt like we found a real home among them.

Of course, with a story like that there's always a "but" waiting. Every single year, Phil and I take some time together to evaluate how we're doing as individuals and as a family in all aspects of life. We talk to the kids about how they're doing, we look at places we could improve, and we talk about what's working well. It's basically a state of the union. We pray for wisdom and we ask God for His guidance for our immediate future. Well on this particular year, both Phil and I realized that we felt stagnant. It had nothing to do with our neighborhood or our friends, who we loved. We just needed a change.

I really wrestled with this decision. We had moved a lot because of Phil's job. Did we really need a change? Or was I just so used to our nomadic life that I just wasn't used to staying put? We'd never had a fear of changing locations, schools, or houses. Phil and I have often said that we're married to each other and our kids, and that's it. We're not married to our jobs or houses. We hold tightly to each other and trust God to lead us to the rest. We haven't been afraid to do life differently, with conviction. To approach life open to following God's purpose, no matter what other people might think or say. People will very seldom understand your decision when it looks different from the way they are living. You will get pushback and maybe even lose some friends. Why? Well when people see you saying "Yes!" to God and following Him enthusiastically, they realize that the lies they've been telling themselves that have allowed them to ignore God's call and stay comfortable just aren't true. The biggest lie they believe? That they have to do everything just like everyone else—*that they have to fit in*. But God didn't make us to fit in, He made us to stand out and stand up for Him. It's not going to be easy, but a life lived chasing God is worth it for you and your family.

We knew we needed a change, but how big of one? Were we looking at a seven mile move? A seventy mile move? Or a seven hundred mile move? Do we change states altogether? I remember asking myself, "How do you know where to go? How do you know what to do? How do you know you are making the right decision?"

And isn't that just life?! Don't we all want *all* the answers before we make the jump? But they wouldn't call it a "leap of faith" if all the answers were there. Phil said to me, "Shannon, sometimes you don't know until after you take a step." Life's biggest decisions cannot be made in fear. They can't be made based on what everyone else thinks or on what everyone else wants. They can't even be made just based on feelings. They have to be made *on faith*. We were taking a leap of faith. That leap of faith was based on trusting that we gain insight about life from the Word of God. Our decision was based in methodical prayer around our decisions and situation. Our leap was based in the unshakeable confidence we had (and still have!) that *God has got this*.

You see, God isn't surprised when you hit a roadblock or a pothole or a little blip on the radar of your life. When those things happen, we have to put our faith into action and rely on God to protect us and guide us through the process of change. When you can wrap your head around the fact that God has got you, then it gives you this freedom to move.

And that's what we did.

THROW AWAY THE BONES

We only moved seven miles away. Looking back, we can totally see His favor in that decision. We couldn't have told you what we were missing, but those needs were met almost immediately once we moved. And now, we can see so clearly the goodness that came to us because we made a decision based on faith in His goodness.

I dove right into our new community. I poured myself into it. I started a new Bible study and over forty women showed up to the very first meeting. The whole experience blossomed into this, "Oh my goodness, I can't believe what God is doing" moment. In fact, a lady I'd never met said to me in that first meeting, "Thank you for doing this. I've lived here for two years and was wondering where my people were." That was such a profound moment for me. God had called me to this community, because it needed me as much as I needed it.

After we left, I was also able to see more clearly all the things we had left behind—all the wonderful, beautiful, soul-affirming stuff that God had done in our lives in the short period of time in that first neighborhood in Austin. It gave me the fortitude to know that, in this new location, I could trust that God was going to do the exact same thing. He was going to meet the needs of my family, no matter how those needs changed. He was going to provide love and care, even if that love and care looked different and new. It was a valuable lesson for our kids too. The lesson that you don't have to do life how everybody else is doing life.

My dad has this great saying: "Eat the meat and throw away the bones," which means that when it comes to what everyone else is doing and saying, take the meat away from it, take the wisdom. But spit out the bones. Leave behind the parts that don't fit. Make a life with God that works for you—outside of others' expectations or ways of doing things. God affords you the grace to change, no matter where you are on your path. Don't be afraid to go a different direction, the direction your heart knows is right for you. Don't be afraid of change. Don't be afraid of the unknown. That is where true freedom is found—the freedom that comes from letting God run wild in your life.

GOD IS IN CONTROL

This all ties back to our girl Esther. Esther trusted God so fully that she was able to be brave, to step into the unknown with complete faith. We will never know, in the moment, why God is working the way he is, but we can trust that God arranges every aspect of our lives for His purposes and His plan. Just as Esther was made queen for "such a time as this" (Esther 4:14), so, too, will you find yourself someday in the right place with the right experiences, connections, and gifts to say "yes!" to God like Esther did, to experience God's promise fulfilled.

Let's take a moment and read Esther 5:9-14.

Here we see Haman plotting to hang Mordecai. It is interesting that in this passage, Haman stands in direct contrast to Esther. When the king asks Esther what favor she wants, she is humble. She does not overextend. She asks that Haman and the king come to a feast that she is preparing. But she does not expose Haman yet. She does not ask the king to kill him. The king says she can basically have half his kingdom, and she takes nothing for herself. She just walks quietly on her path to God.

But Haman in this passage is full of hate. He is completely overextending. He thinks it will be no trouble at all to have Mordecai killed. He is having the gallows built *before he has even asked the king*. He is so confident in his own power, in his own way, that he doesn't think about looking to God. And God, our God, is the one with the plan. God is still in control of this whole mess right now.

Let's take a moment and read Esther 6:1-13.

In this passage, we learn that the king can't sleep. Now I can't help but wonder if God did that on purpose, because in the night hour, the king requests the book of memorable deeds, the chronicles, to be brought to him. And there the king reads that Mordecai was the one responsible for saving him from the plot to overthrow him. So, the king asks, "What has been done for Mordecai," and finds out nothing has been done for him. And, at the exact moment, Haman enters the court to speak to the king.

Talk about timing! And then the conversation shows us what a sense of humor God has. Because as the king is asking Haman what should be done to honor a man who has served him well, Haman is thinking that the king is talking about him. He's listing all the favors that he wants. And the king responds, "Hurry; take the robes and the horse, as you have said, and do so to *Mordecai the Jew"* (Esther 6:10).

Best. Line. Ever.

God worked out every detail. And the order with which he did it is absolutely amazing.

As humans, we are so prideful. We think so much of ourselves. We look inwardly and see only our glories, our triumphs, and our stories. But God sure can get our attention pretty quickly. And that's what's happening with Haman at this point. He was so arrogant and self-centered that he couldn't see past his very own nose. His hate and inability to see outside of his own desires is ultimately his downfall.

Meanwhile, Esther only sees God. She has no idea what is going to happen at any point in this story. She does not try to control even a single detail. In moments when she is called upon to take a stand, stick her stake in the ground, and stand up for her people, she always answers by consulting God first. She fasts. She prays. She looks to Him for guidance. Then she goes forward and does. Not in purposeful plotting, not by manipulating, but in faith. She knows she cannot see the whole picture. She accepts that. Her confidence comes from her blind willingness to follow God, wherever He might be taking her.

As mothers, wives, friends to others, gosh, just as women, it feels like we're hardwired to control things. I'd like to say it's something we can ignore, but it's deep-rooted in us going back generations upon generations. In fact, it goes back as far as the fall in Genesis 3. Eve took control and well, here we all are today! (I'll save that for another Bible study.) If we aren't controlling, sometimes we try to manipulate the situation to fit our needs, our comfort level, and maybe even our ego. Some of this comes from wanting to fit in, be it with our friend group, our community, or at our jobs. It's a problem, ladies, and we're all guilty of it. I'm reminded, in the verses that we are about to read, that Esther could have controlled and manipulated this entire situation. But she didn't. I feel pretty confident that God gave us Esther as a model of how to let go of our need to control and let God do what He does best.

Let's take a moment and read Esther 7:1-10.

This is important. Esther finally reveals Haman's plot. She could have done this so many times throughout this journey, but she didn't. She waited patiently. She followed God to this place where the bigger picture could be seen. God used Esther, a lowly orphan child who was adopted by Mordecai, to save the Jews. It was through her obedience and faithfulness that this plan was seen through.

FIND YOUR PATH

God is working when you can't see Him, or imagine Him, or even begin to comprehend His great and amazing plan. John 3:8 says this, "The wind blows where it wishes, and you hear its sound, but you do not know where it comes from or where it goes. So it is with everyone who is born of the Spirit."

Just as the wind is invisible, so is God. People ask, "How will others ever know if God is working in their life or if He even exists?" If you've ever stepped outside and felt the wind, you've experienced God. He created it and moves it daily into its very existence. His work never stops. He is the breath of life. Just as we feel the wind and see its effects, we too can feel the Holy Spirit working and moving in our own life, if we only pay attention as Esther did.

Let's close this week by throwing out the lie: *You have to fit in* and replacing it instead with the truth: *You have to walk boldly in the path God made for you*. Think about all the times in your life when you were being pushed to go a certain way by the people around you, and instead decided to walk your own path. Think about the blessings that has brought you, the challenges that it has helped you overcome, and the ways in which it brought you closer to the Lord Jesus Christ.

My hope is that my story will inspire you

to find your own unique movement, write your own story with God, and chart your own journey through this crazy twisting and turning world. Everybody's story doesn't have to look the same, but we can take others' experiences as examples to springboard into life in our own way. Just walk closely to God, and the rest will fall into place.

You have to walk boldly in the path God made for you.

Group Study

✦ BIBLICAL EXERCISE:

Have you ever had a Queen Esther moment? Have you felt yourself called to say, do, or serve, and it felt like you were uniquely qualified to answer that call? Was the call challenging to answer? Did it require you to scrap carefully made plans to say "Yes"? Did it require you to sit in uncertainty like Queen Esther? Discuss those moments with each other.

If you haven't had your moment yet, how do you think you might keep an eye out for your "such a time as this"?

QUESTIONS:

- What causes us to believe the lie "You have to fit in"?

- At the root of that lie, there's a strong craving for the acceptance of others. Why do you feel you need others' acceptance?

- What lie are you currently believing that you need to change your mind about?

- Can you have faith in God when you don't have all the answers?

- Are you willing to face opposition for rejecting the lie?

- What will you need to change because you've rejected the lie?

- Why do you think it's so hard to be different in a godly way?

- Does trusting God involve risk?

- What risk might you be taking if you've rejected the lie?

- How has believing the lie brought pain into your life?

 **SCRIPTURE:**

"For a day in your courts is better than a thousand elsewhere. I would rather be a doorkeeper in the house of my God than dwell in the tents of wickedness."

- Psalms 84:10

JOURNAL PROMPT:

In our writing this week, I want you to take a more in-depth look at the last question. How has believing the lie brought pain into your life? Write about the pain or discomfort. Identify where it went wrong. Where do you go from here? Use Esther's story as a template for sharing your thoughts in your writing and remember that your personal walk with Jesus is what's most important.

 **PRAYER:**

God, thank you for allowing us to see Your handiwork all around us, in nature and in life. Allow us to understand that You are working on behalf of all, when we can see it and when we cannot. Build in us the trust to lean on You. Allow us to know that You are dependable for all our needs, and that You will use us, if we are willing. Allow us to follow the conviction of Your Word daily as a guide to life and family, and the relationship between You and us. Allow us to stand firm in Your Word just as Esther did, driving our stakes into the ground with a confidence only You can give. Prick our hearts when we try to control or manipulate, and instead show us how to let go and allow You to proceed for us. For a day in Your courts is better than a thousand elsewhere. No good thing do You withhold from those who walk uprightly. Blessed is the one who trusts in You. Amen.

I am walking with you on this journey.

Love,

Shannon

WEEK FIVE:
"You Just Need to Think Positively"

"When you live by faith, it often feels like you are risking your reputation. You're not. You're risking God's reputation. It's not your faith that is on the line. It's His faithfulness. Why? Because God is the one who made the promise, and He's the only one who can keep it. The battle doesn't belong to you; it belongs to God. And because the battle doesn't belong to you, neither does the glory. God answers prayer to bring glory to His name, the name that is above all names."

— Mark Batterson

"What no eye has seen, nor ear heard, nor the heart of man imagined, what God has prepared for those who love him."

— 1 Corinthians 2:9

Independent Study

REDEFINING POSITIVITY

We are told by self-help books, seven-step experts, and talk show gurus that we need to "believe in ourselves" or "follow these steps and you, too, can live a successful and happy life." We are told, "Positivity = a successful life."

If you're anything like me, I face down this lie almost daily. In today's culture, women are encouraged to be independent, career-minded, and rely only on themselves. Asking for help, especially from a man, can be seen as a sign of weakness. In an attempt to prove to the world that "you have it in yourself to live successfully," most of us find ourselves tackling life's challenges solo. We can overcome obstacles! We can wear multiple hats at one time! We can manufacture success, not only for ourselves but our families as well! Unfortunately, after the weight doesn't come off, our child doesn't make the varsity team, we're not selected to chair a certain event, we don't get to drive with the honor roll bumper sticker on our car—the list goes on and on—we find ourselves worn out, frustrated, and full of questions. It's not until we realize that only God can empower us for a truly purposeful and intentional life, that we can overcome this lie and start seeing true progress.

Saul of Tarsus was busy doing life his way until God got his attention, brought his life to a screeching halt, and spoke true purpose into his heart. From that moment on, Saul, who became known as Paul, grew into a Christian giant whose impact is still felt to this day.

Saul received his early training in a famous Greek university. As was customary in Jewish families, he was raised with Jewish Law, and he went on to study with the greatest Jewish teachers. Saul's family were all Roman citizens, but as Jews, they viewed Jerusalem as the sacred Holy City. All of this training helped Saul advance to a position of authority in religious groups in his thirties, which gave him power. That is when he gained permission from the Jewish authorities to wipe out Christianity. During this process, Saul firmly believed he was acting in the name of God.

Let's take a moment and read Acts 8:1-3.

Saul was a monster to the believers in Jerusalem. He entered house after house, dragging off men and women, and committing them to prison, because they believed Jesus was the Messiah. He terrorized people. But Saul didn't see himself as a monster. He was sincere in what he was doing, believing it to be the will of the Lord. He believed he was acting justly. Saul was lost. He was an over-confident, arrogant bully who had completely misrepresented his religious upbringing and, frankly, didn't have a clue about who the real God was.

We can all relate to this in some form or fashion. All of us have disconnected from the truth at times and haven't wanted to admit it. We constantly struggle and wander, and the entire time we try to look good on the outside. We don't admit our faults or our insecurities. The truth is we each take our own unique winding, twisting path to reach God. Our movement to the cross will probably be a zigzag movement, but God is working in the shadows too.

John 14:6 says, "I am the way, and the truth, and the life. No one comes to the Father except through me." Having a clear understanding of this is essential to the foundation of your relationship with God. Although our paths zigzag, God is leading us to the one door to Him. A builder wouldn't build a house on sand. He would build it on rock to give it a good solid foundation.

Matthew 7:24-25 says, "Everyone then who hears these words of mine and does them will be like a wise man who built his house on the rock. And the rain fell, and the floods came, and the winds blew and beat on that house, but it did not fall, because it had been founded on the rock."

Understanding God and His Word will tether

you to absolute truth.

THE TROUBLE WITH EMOTIONS

Saul's understanding of scripture was that keeping God's law was the way to salvation. He held a false view, believed it wholeheartedly, and was driven by emotion to defend it—even terrorizing those who disagreed. Emotions should only be acted upon when they are based in God's truth.

You can be angry, and that is good, if it's based on truth.

Saul trusted his emotions more than God's Word. He obviously studied scripture in his upbringing, but he was attaching meaning to it based on how he was feeling instead of finding the truth in God's Word and checking his emotions against that truth. How easily things can get twisted if we aren't careful!

I seriously doubt that anyone in this room has been barging into people's houses and sending them to prison for being a Christian. But we still might be guilty of relying on our feelings more than we should. And our emotions might not be based on truth.

As women, we are hard-wired with feelings. We are emotionally intelligent. We feel things strongly. We are keenly aware of what we feel and what others around us feel. But sometimes, our emotions can get off track. We get flooded with too much information, and it becomes hard to tell which emotions are valid, and which emotions are leading us down the wrong path.

God's Word should be the go-to place to bring our emotions back in line. Unfortunately, our culture is bombarding us with the lie that we should be making decisions based on our feelings. If it feels good, then do it. This is a lie and a trap. The truth is that you should only do it if God is at the center of your decision and it aligns with His Word. There are so many verses that are packed with His truth, and we have to read those verses for what they are, not for what we want them to be.

- **Psalm 84:11:** "For the Lord God is a sun and shield; the Lord bestows favor and honor. No good thing does he withhold from those who walk uprightly."
- **2 Timothy 1:13-14:** "So keep at your work, this faith and love rooted in Christ, exactly as I set it out for you. It's as sound as the day you first heard it from me. Guard this precious thing placed in your custody by the Holy Spirit who works in us." (MSG)
- **Colossians 3:2:** "Set your mind on things that are above. Not on things that are on earth."
- **Psalms 119:105:** "Your word is a lamp to my feet and a light to my path."

- **Proverbs 3:5-6:** "Trust in the LORD with all your heart, and do not lean on your own understanding. In all your ways acknowledge him, and he will make straight your paths."

This is where memorization plays a key role. When you memorize God's Word and tuck it away in your heart, you can easily pull it out when you are overwhelmed by emotion and say, "Wait a second, God's Word says whatever is true, whatever is honorable, whatever is pure—those are the things I will focus on. Not how I'm feeling."

You need to think positively and believe in yourself is only true if you have a personal relationship with God and His Word is in your heart. This ensures that your emotions are grounded with a foundation of God's truth. Moving forward like this will help you confidently figure out which decisions you, as a woman, need to make in order to have a holy, loving, and fulfilling life. Relying on God's Word will bring your circumstances into focus, and trusting His Word will lead you in the known and unknown.

SAUL TO PAUL, HIS AWAKENING

The pivotal and climactic moment that changed Saul's life was when he actually met Jesus on the road from Jerusalem to Damascus. He saw Jesus for who He truly was! That's where Saul's journey changed to Paul's transformation. In that moment, he was adopted as God's loving and faithful servant.

Let's take a moment and read Acts 9:1-22.

What a passage! This is what we call transformation by God alone: when a heart as cold as ice experiences a complete transformation in the blink of an eye, where the old passes away and the new takes hold. This moment is Paul's spiritual adoption. Jesus sought him out, and Paul accepted that love, grace, and forgiveness. The scales fell from his eyes, he regained his sight, he rose and was baptized, and he was filled with the Holy Spirit.

Paul had lived his whole life full of himself, but it took only one single moment for the Holy Spirit to enter him. One single decision. And it's the same for every one of us. It's not about living life perfectly. It's about living life imperfectly with Jesus in our hearts and trusting Him. Just like that, Paul's passion in life changed from being a self-righteous persecutor to a compassionate witness of God's grace.

Let's take a moment and read 1 Timothy 1:13-16.

Paul used to persecute, but then he started to preach. That was a miracle!

In life, I've seen people who have said and done horrible things come to know the Lord. And I've seen that same instant transformation in them. I've also seen mean people who lash out in anger and hatred, and I've thought to myself, "If only they knew Jesus." Ladies, surrendering to Him is the only way. This is why all the books and gurus in the world will never have the answers to God's eternal life. They won't, trust me. Their answers are built on emotions and unproven falsehoods. God's truths are built on solid rock.

Let's take a moment and read 2 Corinthians 5:17-21.

This was Paul's passion. To boldly spread the word of Jesus with no fear, fully understanding the harm that could come his way, but at the same time fully putting his stake in the ground and saying, "This is who I am. I was created for this moment. My past does not define me, because I have been redeemed by my Lord." God used Paul's past story, both the bad and the good, to do His work, which has reverberated for generations. That's why Paul is my Bible boyfriend—a stud of a man, that God made whole and new through His son Jesus.

Up until this point, we talked about the physical adoptions of Moses and Esther. But it is so vitally important—a key component to this whole Bible study—to acknowledge that we all must be spiritually adopted. God can save anyone. Paul's story is still being lived out today. The world is filled with tired, lonely, scared, hurting, selfish people. But our God can transform even those hearts.

YOU HAVE IN YOURSELF WHAT IT TAKES

There is nothing—nothing—that makes you feel more like you don't know what you're doing than becoming a parent. From day one, there is so much chaos, uncertainty, fear, and a ton of advice. I had three different births that presented three different challenges. Each really made me come face-to-face with my walk with the Lord in different ways.

When my first child Dru was born, I remember thinking, "This is the only blood I have. It starts and stops with us." I had carried someone nine months inside me and I was so in love with him. At the same time, Dru reminded me of the path that I had journeyed up until that point—my wilderness, peeling back my layers. It had all led me to this moment of holding my flesh and blood in my arms for the first time. The love was more than I could bear. I felt humbled and grateful to have this beautiful little boy in my arms, but it also rekindled the pain inside of me from being abandoned as a baby. Could I truly love him due to my anguish? Could I provide the emotional support even though I was still figuring myself out? These were some of the questions rattling my confidence as a new mom.

I knew there was someone out there who had carried me for nine months. After going through that, she still decided to let me go. I had never understood her decision, but after holding Dru for the first time, it broke my heart all over again. I was so in love with him from the first instant. Hadn't my birth mother felt that way about me? Or maybe I just wasn't loveable. Brad, my pastor, often says that we should mourn births and celebrate deaths. I was bringing my perfect little guy into this nasty world that had just about eaten me up. I wondered, "How do I begin to protect him from the bad stuff just waiting out there?"

But the Holy Spirit was stirring inside of me, even as I worried. I was nudged and reminded to go back to the truth. God was so good. He had opened my eyes to His truths. He had redeemed my heart. He had a plan for me. I knew that He had a plan for Dru too. God was working again on my heart thanks to my precious baby, chipping away at the lies that I had believed for so long.

Two years later, I had my second child, Beau. God had given me a beautiful opportunity to be this little guy's—well, let me rephrase that—this big guy's mommy. Unlike with Dru, this time I didn't feel ready for another child (another lie working its harm inside me). And with Beau, I had a lot more to figure out as a mom.

My son Beau was born full of life. He was such a sweet baby, but at about two years old, I started noticing that certain mile markers that he should have reached developmentally just weren't happening. For example, if I made him a plate of chicken, mashed potatoes, and carrots, he would separate them and eat only the soft mashed potatoes. If he ate a piece of chicken, that poor kid, it was like watching a cow chew its cud. He'd chew it forever and ever and ever, and then he'd choke on it, because he couldn't swallow it. He tripped a lot. Where most kids his age could run and change direction, Beau would do a big circle in order to come back to where he needed to go. He couldn't blow his nose. There were all these little things that I knew in my gut weren't quite right. I knew I needed to bring him to the doctor to have some tests run, to see what was going on.

So many people told me I was worried about nothing. At exactly the moment that my instincts were telling me to look into this, the lie of *"think positive*, it's all good, you're overreacting, he's fine" was growing larger inside me. But I pushed that lie aside and I took Beau to see a doctor.

Sure enough, after having a series of tests run, the doctor told us that Beau was born with a muscle looseness to his body. This didn't fall under any medical condition; it just meant that some muscles in his body just hadn't woken up yet. It broke my heart, because that's what I had been witnessing the whole time. I was seeing this kid spin his paper all the way around, because he didn't have the mobility in his hand to draw a circle like you and I would draw a circle. He put his pen down and then turned the paper to create his circle.

So maybe he had these problems, but also, what a genius, right?! What a fighter! He figured out a way to get his circle in life, and, ever since, he has always had that fighter mentality. Of course, just being a fighter and thinking positive wouldn't have helped Beau. He needed intervention. He was in speech therapy, in physical therapy, in occupational therapy, and in another mobility-based therapy, where he rode horseback to strengthen his core. Now, as a freshman, Beau is about 195 pounds and 6'1". He's as strong as an ox. I mean this kid is something special with his strength. And to see where he started and where he is now is an absolute blessing and miracle all wrapped in one. But it all started with that mommy instinct that I really believe was the Holy Spirit just prompting me, "Hey, you might want to look into that." Just a little whisper in my ear.

Sometimes it can be very difficult to hear the Holy Spirit inside of us over all of the lies the world tells us. The lies are so loud, shouting and clamoring for our attention. The Holy Spirit, at least for me, has always been softer—a whisper, a nudge, a gentle hand. Learning to be still, shut the noise of the lies out, and listen for that truth from the Holy Spirit's whisper is so important. When you can do that regularly it gets easier to listen for the truth of God's unconditional love. Like Paul, you just have to fully accept Him in order to understand His plan for you. I'm not talking about all the details of your journey, but rather having faith in the big picture. You need to have the trust of a little child when it comes to God.

If Beau helped me hear the Holy Spirit's whisper, then it was Sophiann's birth that truly made me understand its importance.

THE BIRTH OF MY DAUGHTER

> *"Now to him who is able to do far more abundantly than all that we ask or think, according to the power at work within us."*
> *- Ephesians 3:20*

As I mentioned in the very first chapter of this book, this is my life verse. And it was the birth of my daughter, Sophiann, that really solidified it inside my heart.

I was sure that I wasn't ever going to have a girl. The boy gene is strong on the Dawson side of the family, and it took thirteen sonograms to convince me that it was actually a girl inside me. I had a routine pregnancy until one night, in my third trimester, I woke up with a strong feeling that I needed to give birth to this little girl in Texas—despite the fact that we were living in Ohio at the time.

It was crazy. I basically woke up in the middle of the night with just the most powerful feeling that the birth *needed* to happen in Texas. There was no reasoning. There was no hard proof. It was just that little whisper of the Holy Spirit. It didn't make sense. We were living in Ohio. Why would we have to complicate everything in order to have this birth take place in Texas? It was crazy that I was feeling this way. Both of my boys were born in Texas, so maybe that's why I was feeling this way? But, no, I wasn't attached to the hospital there or my doctor. I had a great doctor and hospital here in Ohio. I went through every reason I could think of, wanting to make sure it wasn't my hormones talking and it was actually the Holy Spirit. I prayed and surrendered my thoughts over to God, allowing Him to work. He answered by just letting the Holy Spirit sit inside me with that whisper, with that feeling, and I knew I had to go to Texas.

At this point, I was four weeks away from my due date. As soon as my doctor's office opened, I was pounding on the door, with my face smashed up on the glass. The doctor graciously saw me (as if he had a choice in the matter!). He told me I would have to get a sonogram, and that as long as everything looked normal and someone could fly with me, then I could fly to Texas to deliver.

Phil agreed to my crazy plan. He and the boys had to stay back because of football and school obligations. A neighbor and close friend, Cass, insisted that she take the journey with me. She said, "I'm no nurse, but I've delivered four of my own and that has to count for something!" I arrived in Texas safe and sound. I breathed a huge sigh of relief. I wasn't sure why God wanted me in Texas, but I could relax, knowing I had done what He asked of me.

Then my doctor in Texas told me that they needed to do another sonogram at their office, standard procedure to get the lay of the land. As the sonogram technician ran the wand over my belly, he paused. His lips pursed slightly and his brow furrowed. He rotated around a certain area. Something was wrong. He called for the doctor to come and see me immediately.

This was the exact same sonogram I had gotten done a week before. The only difference was that this screen was a large flat monitor on the wall like a TV, whereas the one in Ohio had been a small bedside monitor. The doctor, who had delivered both of my boys, came into that room and greeted me like a friend, but the moment she saw the picture on the screen, her face changed.

"Someone tell me something," I said, panic gripping my heart.

The doctor told me she'd never seen this before, but that I had a low-lying placenta with accreta. A melon-size mass had formed, intertwining two of my major arteries. My doctor told me that some mothers had lived, some babies had lived, but both rarely survived the surgery.

I felt numb and so, so scared. My parents picked me up from the doctor's office, because I couldn't drive home after the shock of that news. Phil got on the next flight to Texas. At the next appointment, the doctor told Phil and I the truth: that my chances of hemorrhaging were high, that the stress of the birth on the baby could kill my daughter.

In the week leading up to the delivery, we prayed so hard. I knew God was still there with me. In my moment of despair, God was still on His throne. I had a choice. I could trust all that I knew was good and sovereign, or I could flee, run, and be angry at the God who created me and Sophiann. Trust me, the flesh wanted to cry out, "This isn't fair! Why me? How could you?" But the truth was, I knew that God had been pointing me towards this exact time in my life, preparing me for this moment, as far back as the first rattle of my insecurities about being adopted. God had been chipping away at my hardened heart to reveal a soft heart beneath, that would hear Him cry out my name in my desperate hour. It was my job, in that moment, to lean into Him and allow Him to carry me through this most difficult time in my life. The only way I could get through was by anchoring myself in Him. Otherwise, I would have been tossed around by the circumstances, feelings, and emotions around me.

I found myself saying, "I'm done listening to the lies."

Right before the surgery, the doctor told Phil that he might have to make a decision about who to save. That he would need an answer ready. I told both Phil and my doctor that, if it came to that, he had to save our baby. I felt such sadness and loss over the idea that I might not see my daughter born or any of my children grow up, but I knew that if I died, I would be going home to my Heavenly Father. I bet you're thinking, "How could she be so matter of fact about that statement?" I had God's peace and that made it possible for me to face my own death. After everything that I had faced in life, in this moment of uncertainty and sadness, I felt the peace that surpasses all understanding. The truth of God's Word was coming alive in me. It was filling in the holes as a solid foundation to hold me up in my darkest hour.

The birth was supposed to be a six-hour surgical procedure, but my daughter was out of me in eleven minutes. I was so relieved to hear her healthy cries, so thankful. But I also knew what they meant. If she was out and OK, then I probably wasn't going to make it. I looked at Phil, tears rolling down my face, and whispered, "I love you. Go be with our daughter. We will see each other again."

But, obviously, I made it through, or I wouldn't be writing this book! God had kept me safe and delivered me to the right doctor to get Sophiann and I through. Guess where I went? Straight to the mountain top. You've heard of mountain top experiences, right? Well I was having one! The whole room that had been around me all night, preparing me for the surgery, changed from the sadness and seriousness of operating, to complete joy. I sang right there in that room. I sang my thanks to God.

In that hour of my daughter's birth, I finally understood God's comprehensive power. That very second, God was able to do more than I had ever asked for or could ever possibly imagine. Positivity wouldn't have gotten me through. Believing in myself doesn't create miracles. All those "You go girl!" inspirational sayings can't fill the holes in anyone's heart. Only God, His love, and His Word can do those things.

THE LESSON OF PAUL

Paul is the absolute embodiment of the truth: "You can and do know what you're doing." Not because he had it all figured out or lived his life perfectly, but because once he saw the truth of God, Paul claimed it absolutely. It didn't matter what harm it did him or that it went against everything that he had stood for in his life up until that point. He didn't care what he looked like or what other people said. He just knew he had to tell the truth of God to the world.

The thing is, that once God is with you, there is no suffering that is too deep. The worst suffering occurs when we reject God. But, like Paul, we have to lay a firm foundation in our life. We have to steep ourselves in God's Word. If you haven't laid a firm foundation at this point in your life as to who Christ is and what He did on the cross for you, what are you going to do when your world is rocked so deeply that you don't know what to do? What are you going to cling to? Who are you going to go to? Who is going to help you in your most desperate time in life? Will you choose faith or fear?

I needed God during Sophiann's birth. I wouldn't have made it without Him. Remember, all our struggles are going to look different. Our moments of need are going to be different. Our journeys are different. But the one common factor is that, if we truly accept Jesus into our hearts and live by His truth, then we can't go wrong. No matter how many dark and twisting paths we travel before we reach Him or how many surprises the future holds. I feel the urgency to shout it from the rooftops, as it's my mission in life to tell everyone of God's unwavering, miraculous, and unending love. I was shouting it for sure the day Sophiann was born to anyone who would listen. And I'm shouting still to this day.

In the words of Paul:

"Finally, brothers, whatever is true, whatever is honorable, whatever is just, whatever is pure, whatever is lovely, whatever is commendable, if there is any excellence, if there is anything worthy of praise, think about these things. What you have learned and received and heard and seen in me—practice these things, and the God of peace will be with you."
- Philippians 4:8-9

A CONVERSATION WITH MY DAUGHTER

To end this chapter, I want to include a conversation that my daughter and I had recently. We were talking about faith. I asked her to define who God was in her own words. How did she see Him?

She said, "When I was at church camp, we had to zip line really high, flying over tall trees and then fall into a freezing cold lake. I was so scared. I even asked my counselor, 'Has anyone died on this thing?' Mom, my heart was racing and I was sweating. My whole body was shaking. My counselor said, 'Step out. I promise it will hold you, and you will fly.' I stepped off the ledge, and, in an instant, Mom, I knew I was being held to the line. My fear was replaced with joy, and peace, and excitement. I was flying, and it felt so incredible. Then I belly flopped into the water and quickly went under. But I had a life vest on, so I popped right back up."

This is faith. Believing, trusting, moving towards Jesus in your relationship with Him, and getting to feel what it's like to fly. The belly flops in life hurt. We all sin and make bad choices. We all get pulled under by life things, but God is quickly there to pop us back up and rescue us from that. Through His grace. It's not by our works or positive attitudes, but by His grace that we are saved.

We can trust that His lifeline, like the zip line, will always be there, solid and secure, holding us to Him. It's when our personal life doesn't align with God's Word that we go from flying on a zip line to teetering on a tightrope. You can't have peace until you understand God's unmerited grace.

Paul understood this, and we all can too.

**Listen to your gut.
You can and do know what
you're doing.**

Group Study

✦ BIBLICAL EXERCISE:

Let's talk about feelings! We all experience a wide range of emotions on any given day, from peace during our morning quiet time with God, to frustration when our kids can't seem to get out the door for school without losing every possession they've ever owned, to annoyance when we get cut off in traffic, to joy when our whole family sits down together for dinner at the end of the day. So how do we know which emotions to trust and act on, and which to ignore? Let's discuss times when acting on our emotions got us into trouble.

What are some verses that help you push past your emotions and rely on God's truth instead?

QUESTIONS:

- Have you ever felt unequipped or inadequate for a task?

- What factors led you to feel this way?

- What do all "self-help" programs have in common?

- Why can't people establish themselves before God as righteous?

- What is the biggest challenge you face right now?

- What can you do to face this challenge?

- What can you do when God doesn't seem to be listening?

- What did Saul do with challenges before he met Jesus?

- What challenges did Paul face after Jesus found him?

- Why do you think we have so much trouble trusting God?

 **SCRIPTURE:**

"Trust in the Lord with all your heart, and do not lean on your own understanding."

- Proverbs 3:5

JOURNAL PROMPT:

Write a letter to God describing your past failures, your current hang-ups, and your unknown future. Link that to the continued story you've already begun in early chapters. See how it all ties together. End your writing in thanksgiving. Thank God for this moment in time, just like Paul did when the scales fell from his eyes. See what God has done and will do in this personal awakening and be sure to trust in Him and not on your own understanding.

 **PRAYER:**

God, first, thank you for all that You have done and will do. You're the founder of each of us; we are uniquely designed by Your hands. We give You all the glory and honor. I know this life is hard, with many ups and downs. Father, make it abundantly clear that we can trust You. Allow us to lean on You in our darkest hours. That we can call on You and, in a second, You will be there. That You desire an intimate relationship with each of us, no matter what we've done. Like Paul, we, too, can be transformed in a second. Living a life that would be pleasing and honoring to You. God create in us a new desire to want You more. Give us boldness to stand up for You, spreading the love of Your gospel to those around us, through our own story. Work in us and through us by Your mighty hand. Amen.

I'm walking with you on this journey.

Love,

Shannon

WEEK SIX:
"You Are Unloveable"

"The most amazing verse in the Bible is John 3:16. No one can ever explain the 'Why' of 'For God so Loved.' The only possible answer is because God is Love, and He chose to."

- Ken Sheppard[9]

"For God so loved the world, that he gave his only Son, that whoever believes in him should not perish but have eternal life."

- John 3:16

Independent Study

PAUL'S JOURNEY

I am someone who saw myself as unlovable for most of my life. This was not because of the people around me. I was loved by my family, by my friends, and then by my husband, who saw so much in me. But I felt unlovable. I mean, deeply unlovable. A hole had been left in my heart by a birth mother, who chose to leave me behind, and that emptiness followed me wherever I went. Through adoption, through marriage, through births—year after year—the lie that I was unlovable somehow became my biggest truth. It pushed me further away from God than anything else ever has. I believed in Him. I had accepted Him. But I felt like there was just this gap between us caused by that lie. Believing that lie kept me from trusting God fully.

You are unlovable is the most harmful lie of them all. It does the most damage. It creates a void inside that cannot be filled by anything, because it's a void that keeps God out. If we can't love and accept ourselves, if we can't find redemption in ourselves, then how can we lovingly serve God, who created us exactly as we are? How can we sing of His grace and beauty? We need to own the truth that God does not make anyone unlovable. We need to see that grace and beauty reflected in our own hearts. We need to recognize it in our own stories. Only then can we truly be servants to the Lord.

This is part of the reason that I really admire Paul's journey. Paul understood that his struggles served to spread the gospel of Jesus Christ. Here was a person who had committed the most horrible crimes, and yet in Jesus Christ he found redemption. He found purpose. He found a second chance. He found love for himself, no matter what had happened in his life before that point.

Let's take a moment and read Philippians 1:12-30.

Here, Paul is stating that his struggles ultimately helped him preach the gospel. This is a man who found worth in himself, given to him by God's grace. He found love for others, because he found love in Jesus. He might have done everything wrong at first. But, ultimately, he used his journey to teach others about the unconditional love and salvation of Jesus Christ. He turned his worst moments into tools for spreading Jesus's love.

You and I are here to do that exact same thing.

I mentioned this before, but I hesitated to write this Bible study. I believed every single one of these lies at some point. I felt unworthy. I felt insecure. I felt unlovable. I grew afraid that people would read this just to get the scoop on my personal life. But this book was not written for curious minds. This book was written for two reasons:

1) To share my journey as an example for others who are looking to bridge the gap between where they are and where they need to be with the Lord. It is so important to know who God is. Maybe you have accepted Christ but there is just this distance caused by the lies that you believe. And that's what this book is for. Because I felt that distance at one point too. We all do. I was a pastor's kid, for crying out loud, I still believed these lies. I'm hoping my journey will help you reject the lies of the world and instead accept the unbelievable love of our Lord.

2) I'm also writing this for those who might not really know who Jesus is. I'm praying that, through this book, God will bring you to Him. My hope is that God will prick and nudge your heart to a point where you know, without a doubt, that you are loved beyond measure. You were created by God and He knows that there is something special inside of you. He wants you to understand who He is and accept the free gift. It's that simple.

Our journeys can inspire one another. Our transformations can save one another. Our examples can encourage one another. Just as Paul preached God's salvation, so, too, can we. This is our testimony. And this is my journey. My miracle. How I learned to love myself fully.

MY BIRTH STORY

Do you remember that stranger I met on the football field? The one who called me and simply said, "I have the information you've wanted for your entire life." Well it turns out, he was right.

I burst into tears when I got that call. And then he told me the story of my birth mom: In 1971, in the deep south, a seventeen-year-old unwed girl named Debra discovered she was pregnant. I can only imagine the thoughts and the fears that flooded her head. Shame, embarrassment, guilt, probably anger. She was only seventeen, but she was brave enough to ask her parents and doctor for counsel on what to do with the baby. She felt strongly that she wasn't ready to handle the responsibility of having a child, but the doctor became her friend and he urged her to give the child up for adoption instead of terminating the pregnancy.

Debra resisted. She was headstrong and stubborn. Once her mind was made up, that was usually it. But the doctor found a women's center about an hour away that would allow her to stay there through her pregnancy, learn a trade, and then have the baby under their care, as long as she agreed to give the child up for adoption. Debra decided to give it a chance.

Debra's parents wanted her to keep the baby. They made the drive up to the women's center every weekend to visit her. They begged and pleaded with Debra to come home, have the baby, and stay with them. They wanted to help her raise her daughter and be a mom. Debra told her mom to stay away, because Debra knew if her mom saw the baby, she'd want to keep it. But on the day that Debra was giving birth, she called her mom and asked her to drive up. She needed her there.

Debra's mom got in the car immediately and drove the road that she knew so well to the center, but a sudden unexpected storm stopped her. She had to pull over. By the time she made it to the center, Debra and the baby (me!) were no longer in the delivery room. The two of us had been separated in an instant. Think hard about this: the months of feeling her baby grow and move inside of her, the hours of labor, the pain and exhaustion, then the birth, seeing a healthy baby that looked so much like her, knowing all along that her decision had already been made. That her baby girl would be placed into the arms of a stranger, another woman who she would call mommy, who would love and raise her. It gets me every time. Having now grown and birthed three babies, I understand exactly how difficult it was for Debra to choose life and then make the painful sacrifice to hand me to another family because she wanted the best life possible for me. I get emotional when I think of the mighty hand of God in this entire situation. He formed my inner parts and knitted me together in my mother's womb. My frame was not hidden from Him when I was being made in secret. God saw my unformed substance. He worked within Debra's heart and body to make me.

The delivery nurse really had a soft spot for Debra. If my mother was anything like me, they probably became friends during her stay there. There was a rule in place during the adoption that nothing tangible from the baby was to leave with the mother after giving birth. But the nurse made an exception for Debra. The nurse gave my mother the diaper pin from the first cloth diaper I wore. Debra wore that pin her entire life, to remind herself that she had given her baby a better life than she could have ever possibly provided her. It was an act of love, not of abandonment. I wasn't unlovable. I was loved so deeply, that my mother accepted a life filled with the pain of not knowing me so that I could have a life of promise. My mom hadn't seen something wrong in me. My mother had seen potential in me.

On November 14, 1978, Debra was involved in a horrific car accident. A friend was following her on a road that was wet and dark, and, suddenly, Debra lost control of her car. She was seriously injured. Debra's friend knew about the diaper pin that Debra wore and retrieved it before the paramedics arrived. Debra died shortly after arriving at the hospital.

When I heard this story, a deep sadness washed over me. My heart was broken. I had asked for years for my prayers to be answered, but I never imagined this could be the outcome. I told Phil I needed to meet Debra's parents, my grandparents. I needed to know more.

I still remember walking up to my grandmother, my flesh and blood. I remember looking into her eyes for the first time and knowing, beyond a shadow of a doubt, that I was her granddaughter. She knew it, too. It felt like a Hallmark movie moment. We cried, and hugged, and cried some more—years of built-up emotion released in one meeting. Then, my grandmother put the diaper pin in my hand and wrapped my fingers around it. As I stared through my tears, I heard her say, "She would want you to have this now." That pin was a physical reminder of how much my mother had loved me. A symbol I could hold onto to combat the lie I'd told myself for so long, the lie that I wasn't loveable.

We spent the day catching up on years of life

lived. We discovered a million crazy coincidences. For example, the place where I met my husband? My aunt had been sitting in that audience at a previous show! She said she'd been watching me intently, although at the time she didn't understand why.

It was right in that moment that I knew how intricately God had orchestrated every detail of my life because of how much He loved me. I thought I had been abandoned, but I had been handed over to a better life. I thought no one wanted me, but there was a whole family who had been ready to accept me. I thought I wasn't loved, but I was loved more than I could have ever imagined. By my birth mother, my adopted parents, and, most of all, by God.

Only through God's miraculous plan did I fully see a mother's love for her child, and a child's love for her mother—a mother she had never met.

PUTTING ON THE NEW SELF

This was such a wakeup call in my life. For years, I hadn't been able to connect fully with myself or with God. I did all the right things. I went through all the right motions, but something had always felt off because I didn't believe I was worthy of love. The discovery of my birth family and my birth mom's story changed all of that. I found a love for myself that I didn't think was possible. And it was then that I knew I had to wake up. If I believed my birth family and all they had done to give me a better life. If I believed Phil when he said that, one day, I'd see myself as he saw me. If I believed my children, who were my own flesh and blood, who I loved beyond measure and who returned that love. Then I had to find myself lovable. I had to fully immerse myself in the immense, incredible love God had always been holding out to me.

Let's take a moment and read Colossians 3:1-17.

I love how this passage ends:

"And above all these put on love, which binds everything together in perfect harmony. And let the peace of Christ rule in your hearts, to which indeed you were called in one body. And be thankful. Let the word of Christ dwell in you richly, teaching and admonishing one another in all wisdom, singing psalms and hymns and spiritual songs, with thankfulness in your hearts to God. And whatever you do, in word or deed, do everything in the name of the Lord Jesus, giving thanks to God the Father through him."

These are Paul's words. Our societies, our lives, our circumstances are so very different, yet, thousands of years later, they are exactly applicable to my life. And to yours too. That is the miracle of the gospel. God's Word is timeless. It doesn't matter when it was written, you can read God's Word today and the words will apply to your life. God's Word was written for you, to be stored in your heart, to awaken God's love in your soul, and to show you that you are loveable.

- Can you think of how the above verses apply to your life at this very moment?

- Imagine if you were to love and accept every part of yourself—even your struggles, even your mistakes—wholly and completely. How would your life change?

- What would your new self look like? What could she do?

Paul's spiritual awakening was the transformation from non-believer to a believer. In my awakening, I was already a believer. But God caught my attention with both Sophiann's birth and the discovery of my birth mother's story. And it transformed my life afterwards. I had felt God so unmistakably by my side in that delivery room; it was the catalyst for my spiritual awakening. I had already accepted Jesus into my heart. But now I was learning to love and accept myself, and that was bringing me closer and closer to God.

At that point, Paul's teachings really came alive for me. That's why I think Paul is so important in my life. Because all the books I read by him, be it Acts, Ephesians, Philippians, or Romans, feel like letters written straight to me. Letters written straight to all of us.

It is *God's truth* that ultimately destroys *the world's lies*.

You are loved.

Group Study

✦ BIBLICAL EXERCISE:

Let's talk about love. We all feel loved when a friend remembers our birthday, or a co-worker buys our coffee, or our kids give us big hugs. But we often don't take as much notice of God's love in our life. When a prayer is answered or a difficult situation just happens to work out perfectly, do we take the time to stop and thank God? Let's discuss ways God shows His love for us in small ways. How can we work to be intentional about noticing and thanking Him when we see them?

QUESTIONS:

- When people feel unloved, they often compensate to make others like them more. What are some of the ways that people do this?

- Others compensate by becoming "invisible," flying under the radar or finding other ways to stay out of the limelight. Give examples.

- What word describes where you are in your journey after reading this chapter? Is it unloveable or something else?

- Do you think Saul was sincere in believing that he was doing God's will in persecuting Christians?

- Is sincerity enough to earn God's favor?

- When, and in what ways, have you struggled with feeling unloved?

- Where do you turn when things go wrong or the unexpected happens? Why?

- Is salvation knowing a set of truth's or having a relationship with Christ?

- What did it cost Paul to trust and embrace Christ and become a follower?

- Answer honestly the most important question asked: Do you have a personal relationship with Jesus? If "Yes," then explain where you go from here. If "No", ask yourself why you don't and where you go from here.

SCRIPTURE:

"See what kind of love the Father has given to us, that we should be called children of God; and so we are."

- 1 John 3:1

✎ JOURNAL PROMPT:

Take a look back at the story you've written in your journal in response to these prompts. What do you want the ending to be? I know my ending will be Heaven, surrounded by God's love. But I don't want to wait for that feeling. I want to feel surrounded by God's love every minute of every day. I want you to identify the blocks in your life that are keeping you from feeling that love. These might be your own self-doubt, guilt about your past, your own feelings, or even just getting caught up in the mundane details of each day. Let's reflect on how we can actively push those things aside and bask in the love God offers each of us. When we can understand who God is, then we can start to see the great love He has for us, His children. Then your faith begins to take on a personal relationship. His death for your sin = His redeeming love.

 **PRAYER:**

Father, as we close the page on this book, I pray that the heart will awake to you, our Redeemer. Allowing Your Word to penetrate our marrow and make us new. Either new in Christ for the first time or a do over in our faith. That we understand that You declare Your righteousness on us at salvation, our faith and our journey progressively makes us righteous, still as sinners. And that one day we will be one hundred percent righteous in the sight of Your face. May we lean on Your goodness, Your sovereignty, Your wisdom, Your holiness, Your faithfulness, and Your love for us every hour we draw a breath. In Your wonderful name, Jesus. Amen.

I'm walking with you on this journey.

Love,

Shannon

CONCLUSION:
SEEK TRUTH

Conclusion: Seek Truth

To understand how God's words can work miracles in our life, let's take a look at Romans. Saul was intimately acquainted with how the lies of the world can blind us to God's truth, so Paul worked diligently to spread that truth to anyone he could. These letters from Paul are full of truth, those little markers that can just steer you back to your path with God. And it's so important that we seek the truth in God's Word and hold it close, to combat the lies all around us.

> "For all have sinned and fall short of the glory of God."
> - Romans 3:23

Notice the *all* in this statement. It doesn't say some, which is really important. It doesn't say some people are good and some people are bad. Some people sin and some don't. No. It says *all*. All have sinned and fall short. We all fall short of being perfect, because there's only one perfect being and that's God. But His standard is perfection, so what can we do?

> "But God shows his love for us in that while we were sinners, Christ died for us."
> - Romans 5:8

Despite our flaws, despite our sins, Christ loves us. He chose to pay the penalty for our sins because of that great love. Listen to the words here. For us. While we were still sinners, Christ died for us. He knew our sinful nature. He knew what He was dying for. He made us His choice anyway. How blessed are we. What a miracle, to have this merciful God!

> "Therefore, since we have been justified by faith, we have peace with God through our Lord Jesus Christ."
> - Romans 5:1

We come to God in faith, trusting in the resurrected, living Christ as our Savior. God, right then and there, declares us to possess Christ's righteousness. We begin our Christian life. Though we have a righteous standing before Him and are adopted as His children, we still are imperfect and sinful and we need to grow spiritually. That is how we stand before Christ. His righteousness is credited to us!

> "For our sake he made him to be sin who knew no sin, so that in him we might become the righteousness of God."
> - 2 Corinthians 5:21

If you don't get anything else from this Bible study, I want you to accept the following three very important truths, truths that are essential to understanding your walk with the Lord.

TRUTH #1: JUSTIFICATION

God begins our journey of faith through offering us the undeserved/unattainable forgiveness of our sins.

Imagine you're broke. There is no way to pay your bills. You have tried, but failed to make ends meet. One day, your banker calls and informs you that someone has gifted you a tremendous inheritance and access to all that he has. You've gone from broke to wealthy, instantaneously. You did not earn this gift, nor did you deserve it. This is exactly what happens when you accept Jesus as your Savior. God offers forgiveness of your sins. Once you accept what God has done for you, the Bible says God transforms your position before Him. You transform from an unforgiven sinner headed to eternal death, to a forgiven sinner now headed to eternal life. This happens instantaneously. This is God's great gift to you, one that you and I do not deserve, nor can earn.

> "...yet we know that a person is not justified by works of the law but through faith in Jesus Christ, so we also have believed in Christ Jesus, in order to be justified by faith in Christ and not by works of the law, because by works of the law no one will be justified."
> - Galatians 2:16

TRUTH #2: SANCTIFICATION

God guides us on our journey of faith, as we grow and mature, becoming more like Him.

Unlike justification, which is instantaneous, sanctification is ongoing. Now that you are a forgiven sinner, God sends his Holy Spirit to you to guide you through this new journey of faith. You will learn about God's truth in this phase. You will learn new godly habits as you break free from old sinful ones as well. I wish I could tell you we will never sin again nor struggle, but we all begin this journey as spiritual infants in need of instruction, discipline, and care. As we learn to follow the instruction of the Holy Spirit, we become more like Christ. We will never fully become perfect here on earth, but certainly now have the ultimate guide to point us in the right direction, giving us an opportunity to represent God in our life here on earth.

> "And I am sure of this, that he who began a good work in you will bring it to completion at the day of Jesus Christ."
> - Philippians 1:6

TRUTH #3: GLORIFICATION

God finishes our journey and we are made sinless with Him in heaven.

One day, our life will be over. The justified forgiven sinner, will now be made perfect. There will be no more sin struggles, burdens, fear, sickness, pain or regret. Our sanctification will now be complete. We will be with the One who started it all for us, and led us along the way. We will be in heaven with Him!

> "For the wages of sin is death, but the free gift of God is eternal life in Christ Jesus our Lord."
> - Romans 6:23

Accepting Christ and His righteousness doesn't mean that it doesn't matter if we sin. It does. And there are still consequences to our sin. If you're caught, there will be outward consequences. If you're not, you live with those consequences inwardly. But God can take that burden from you. Our flesh is a powerful thing. Our natural tendency is to leave God out and to do it our own way. We must acknowledge that and remember to turn to God and ask Him to take those burdens from us.

> "And we know that for those who love God all things work together for good, for those who are called according to his purpose. For those whom he foreknew he also predestined to be conformed to the image of his Son, in order that he might be the firstborn among many brothers. And those whom he predestined he also called, and those whom he called he also justified, and those whom he justified he also glorified."
> - Romans 8:28-30

We are all aiming to be like Jesus, but we all fall so terribly short. We are all onions, and once our layers are pulled back, we all stink. Even you, who follow Jesus. Even you, who don't know who Jesus is. You stink. You need God's help. You need a Savior. Just like I stink. And I need a Savior.

> "There is therefore now no condemnation for those who are in Christ Jesus. For the law of the Spirit of life has set you free in Christ Jesus from the law of sin and death. For God has done what the law, weakened by the flesh, could not do. By sending his own Son in the likeness of sinful flesh and for sin, he condemned sin in the flesh, in order that the righteous requirement of the law might be fulfilled in us, who walk not according to the flesh but according to the Spirit. For those who live according to the flesh set their minds on the things of the flesh, but those who live according to the Spirit set their minds on the things of the Spirit. For to set the mind on the flesh is death, but to set the mind on the Spirit is life and peace. For the mind that is set on the flesh is hostile to God, for it does not submit to God's law; indeed, it cannot. Those who are in the flesh cannot please God. You, however, are not in the flesh but in the Spirit, if in fact the Spirit of God dwells in you. Anyone who does not have the

> **Spirit of Christ does not belong to him. But if Christ is in you, although the body is dead because of sin, the Spirit is life because of righteousness. If the Spirit of him who raised Jesus from the dead dwells in you, he who raised Christ Jesus from the dead will also give life to your mortal bodies through his Spirit who dwells in you."**
>
> **- Romans 8:1-11**

This is life. This is gospel. If you set your eyes on the things of this world, if you are listening to the advice of the world, if Google is getting more action than God, then you are turning to the flesh. And the flesh always lies. The flesh brings eternal death. But to set your mind on the Spirit is a life of truth, a life of peace. You have to go to God's Word. You have to step into His spotlight. You have to put your eyes on God and allow Him to be the anchor of your life. That will bring you eternal life and peace. For the mind that is set on the flesh is hostile to God.

Sometimes, we lose our balance. We waver and wobble, like I did, because the world is pulling us one way, but God's words are gently leading us another. If Jesus lives in you and your heart is open to Him, then you are more likely to recognize those nudges.

You might be asking, "Well okay, Shannon. How do I even do this? How can I begin to have a personal relationship with Jesus?"

> **"Because, if you confess with your mouth that Jesus is Lord and believe in your heart that God raised him from the dead, you will be saved."**
>
> **- Romans 10:9**

There it is. It's that simple. It's confessing that you are a sinner and accepting what Jesus did for you on the cross. By accepting what Jesus did for you on the cross, we can all accept the inevitability of death. When Jesus rose from the dead, He was set apart. His words are true. We can trust in the truth of His words, so we can trust that He will return! After you have declared Jesus as your Savior, nothing can ever separate you from the love of God.

I believe that access to God is always available. He is there in a second. In a split second. I don't care if you've been separated from Him for ten years, twenty years, seventy-five years. All you have to do is cry out to Him. All you have to do is say, "God, I messed up. I'm asking that you forgive me. And mend this relationship. Because I desperately want it."

Don't be afraid or embarrassed to reach out to the one who created you. He's waiting for such a time as now. Don't allow the lies that you are unlovable, unworthy, or that you have to do something to run from your past take residence any more. Break free of those and allow God to breathe truth and life back into you.

- **With God, you are enough.**
- **Look back at your life.** Study its lessons, even the pain and heartbreak. Use those lessons to draw yourself closer to God's love and His glory.
- **Accept Jesus into your heart as your Savior and begin making him Lord of your life.** That's your only responsibility. You do not have to do anything to please others. Instead, learn to lead others to God through your story.
- **You will always fit in with the Lord.** He has always been there waiting for you to call out to Him. You don't have to do anything to fit in with Him, except be humble enough to accept Him, and accept that He knows your life even better than you do. He is never surprised by struggles and trials. He allows them to draw you to Him and uses them to refine you.
- **You know what you're doing.** You have the truth of God

inside you. Sometimes, you just need to be brave enough to use it. Let go of your insecurities. Let go of your doubt. If you are following God, then those things are just lies trying to draw you away from Him. You've got this.

- **Because you are lovable.** God made you. He knows exactly what He put inside you. He knew you long before you were born. You are His ambassador of love. You are the reason He sacrificed His son. Knowing God loves you that much is what makes you worthy and able to love Him back. You are worthy!

This is God's truth. Now go out and tell others about this miracle. About your specific miracle. It might be scary, humbling, and difficult. But it's your path to the cross. And it won't look like anyone else's.

So, this is my story. It's still unfolding before me, day by day, but thankfully, I already know how it will end. God has already triumphed over the lies of the world and He will be victorious in my life, too, because I've already given my life to Him. Some days I still struggle with the same lies, but God is faithful in showing me the truth. He'll be faithful to you too!

His plan, my story, His glory!

In His Amazing Grace,

Shannon

Leading Your Own Bible Study

One of my biggest leaps toward God took place when I started to lead Bible studies in my own home. They gave me a deeper understanding of God's Word, and I got to see, firsthand, how God's Word was absolutely transforming the lives of the people around me. If you want to know the miracle of Jesus, sit in a room full of women. There is so much to learn in this space!

Being at the front of the room does *not* mean you are teaching and everyone else is learning. No way! I learn more from the women in my studies than the other way around. Every time someone tells me their story, it just floors me. Jesus is working in someone else's life, and, through them sharing, Jesus is teaching me more about how He works in my own life.

Basically, my responsibility as a Bible study leader is to provide a space where women can learn from one another and lead one another closer to Jesus Christ. And that's what Bible studies are for. They are a place for each of us to see one another, to learn from one another, and to grow together in God's Word. Then, we need to be the feet of Jesus out there in our own circles, spreading that same understanding to the people we rub shoulders with every day.

So, here are a few tips for taking your first step toward leading your own Bible study, if you feel Jesus moving you to do this.

DON'T FEEL LIKE YOU CAN'T LEAD

Like I mentioned in the first chapter, I am an insecure leader. The biggest challenge that I ever overcame in leading Bible studies was just getting the nerve to do it in the first place. I mess up words all the time—when I am speaking and when I am writing—and that will never change no matter how many Bible studies I teach. But I don't let that stop me! You don't need to be perfect to lead. If anything, a few little mistakes can sometimes make other people feel more comfortable. When they know they aren't dealing with someone perfect, they can find the courage to accept their own imperfections. And a few layers peeled back on the onion later, we are all speaking our absolute messy truths to one another. And that's where the real work gets done.

As a woman, it's important to take a leadership positions in your community. And to give other women around you the confidence to do the same. There's a time to be led, and then there's a time to lead. Don't be afraid to step up when it's your time. Start with a single friend over coffee at your kitchen counter. Then invite enough people to fill your dining room table. When you're ready, ask those people to each invite a friend and move the group to your family room. You're not only building your own confidence, you're serving others and allowing His perfect design to work through you. You can do this!

TAKE A PULSE ON THE ROOM

You need to try to read the room before you start a Bible study on any given week. That's talking to ones you trust, asking about new ladies, or trying to get a brief background on the new people before study starts. You won't get to everyone. It takes time. Be flexible in your lesson. Speak truth always, but maybe come in the back door instead of barging in the front. My Bible boyfriend understood this! Paul was great at reading rooms. Just take a look at Acts 17:22-34.

FOSTER A SENSE OF SAFETY

You can't lead a successful Bible study if every person in the room feels guarded and on edge. We are messy people. We have messy truths to tell. And there is no way we are going to tell them if we feel like we are sitting in a room of judgment. *What's shared in Bible study, stays in Bible study.* Really stress this! Also, stress that this is not a place for spouse bashing, strife, or gossip wrapped up in real pretty words like *"we need to pray for."*

Foster a sense of safety and acceptance in your room. Maybe tell a story of yours that shows just how flawed you are, so others will have the courage to do the same. Immediately shut down any negative or disparaging comments from people in the room. Anyone who is acting perfect while everyone else admits they are not, well, that is the person you need to take out to coffee for a heart-to-heart. See what they are really struggling with, love and help them, but don't let their negativity affect others.

IT NEVER HURTS TO HAVE A GOOD WINGMAN

Anyone who has ever had to lead a Bible study knows about the *dreaded silence.* You know what I mean, the kind of silence that is so silent it actually seems like the loudest thing you'll hear all day. It can cause your heart to drop, your train of thought to completely disappear, and your words to get all tied up in your head. For these occasions, it's good to have a wingman. Someone in the room who is an ally and friend, and who isn't afraid to jump in when the dreaded silence hits.

LISTEN, SHARE, AND WRITE

I cannot stress the importance of writing things down. Whether it's pre-set journal prompts or maybe just a moment of reflection that you came up with spontaneously that you want every person in the room to spend some time thinking about. This writing time can really inspire everyone.

Writing things down can allow for a private practice in a public space. It can help people organize their thoughts, which will ultimately lead to richer conversations once you do start sharing. Speaking of sharing, I strongly suggest finding one or two women that have written out their story and are willing to share it with the group. This can be the sweetest time for an amazing conclusion to this study—maybe a Week 7 if it seems fitting.

EMBRACE YOUR CREATIVITY

Do question and answer sessions. Go off book. Throw in some fun activities that you think can help people connect to the text. Don't limit yourself just to the chapter in front of you. A Bible study should be an open and organic space. Bring your creativity as a leader to it.

Don't worry. Even if you follow these tips perfectly, you are going to mess up. And that imperfect moment is often the perfect opportunity for Jesus to sweep in and take over. You and Jesus have got this! Now get out there and lead!

I'm walking with you on this journey,

Shannon

Acknowledgments

This book would not be possible if it weren't for Debra and her commitment to me, her unborn baby girl. It always starts with a choice. Hers was a life for me. I am so thankful for the good and the bad. If it all was for this very moment, then such a time is this!

To Amber and Esther—I thank God for bringing us all together. Thank you for your persistent encouragement to write my story.

To all my girls, you know who you are, who committed to pray for this project daily and for the future readers. I couldn't have done it without all of you standing alongside me through this journey.

To all the Bible study ladies from past years and to my current study. Seeing your growth and love for Jesus, is truly a blessing to me. To Brad, my pastor and teacher of God's Word. Your knowledge of the Bible overflows to truth that can be understood and then applied every week.

To my parents, Ken and Billie for praying me through this process. Thank you for being available to listen when I hit a roadblock or had a question. Thank you for extending immeasurable love as always. Dad, your biblical wisdom is beyond my comprehension at times, but your way of teaching is always understandable and spot on—never watered down. Thank you for showing me how to reach the lost, encourage the weary, and to love all.

To my kids —thank you for your constant encouragement and excitement to write. Being your mom is the best job ever!

To Phil encouraging me, "there will never be the perfect time, so write." Thank you for letting me grow into the person I was created to be. Thank you for being patient with me and for loving me when I know I was a hot mess at times. Thank you for your commitment to this marriage, striving to be different, but not perfect. Who would have thought, on the stage of Johnnie High, we would meet and travel a road such as this. I love you more than these words can write. His Plan, Our Story, His Glory!

Endnotes

[1] Oswald Chambers, *My Utmost for His Highest* (Discovery House, 1992)

[2] Oswald Chambers, *The Love of God: An Intimate Look at the Father-Heart of God* (Discovery House, 2015)

[3] Brennan Manning, *The Ragamuffin Gospel: Good News for the Bedraggled, Beat-Up, and Burnt Out* (Multnomah, 2005)

[4] Chip Ingram, *The Real God* (Baker Books, 2004, 2011)

[5] Oswald Chambers, *The Highest Good with The Pilgrim's Song Book and Thy Great Redemption* (Discovery House, 2015)

[6] Mark Batterson, *The Circle Maker* (Zondervan, 2011)

[7] Ken Sheppard, my dad.

notes

notes

notes

notes

notes

notes

notes

notes

notes

notes

notes

notes

notes

notes

notes

notes

notes